W9-CUH-787

HOLIDAYS &PARTIES

Compiled by
**Professional Home Economics &
Family and Consumer Science Teachers
of California, Nevada, Arizona, and Utah**

Editor
Gerry Murry Henderson

Graphic Design, Typography, and Production
Mike Burk Production Services, Long Beach, CA

Library of Congress Catalog
Card No. 83-072757
ISBN 0-914159-19-4

HOLIDAYS & PARTIES

Everybody loves Holidays! Fun, festive, family, friendship occasions – all call for good food and great recipes!

The **Main Credit** for the content of this book belongs to the **Home Economics & FACS Teachers** of California, Nevada, Arizona, and Utah! They are the "culinary artists" whose recipes make these books possible (their names and schools are beneath each recipe).

Further Thanks to the following people, without whose help this book would not be:

- **Nancy Freeman,** of Fullerton, who patiently receives, edits, and types all these recipes into the computer.

- **Gerry Henderson,** of Temple City High School, who "tracks" each and every recipe to make sure it's perfect.

- **Doug Herrema,** of Huntington Beach, our Publication Manager, who plans each book and obtains the beautiful photography for each cookbook.

- **Doug Pierce,** of Los Angeles, who personally collects more recipes than any of us.

- **Mike Burk,** of Long Beach, who designs the cover and photos, and then "flows" the entire book! Thank you again Mike, for somehow finding time to do our books!

- **Jerry Bernstein** and **Lisa Kline,** of KNI, Inc., in Anaheim, have proved for the past fourteen years that they are "printing professionals"!

- **Bill "Rich" Richardson**, **Roger Uppermann** and **Bob Mauthe,** each drive many miles and many hours to distribute and pick-up these books from schools, who sell them via students as fundraisers.

- Many foods companies and councils contributed the beautiful photography within this book, and **we thank them so much: Lawry's Foods** of Monrovia, CA; **Hershey Foods** of Hershey, PA; **Pillsbury Company** of Minneapolis, MN; **National Pork Board** of Des Moines, IA.

And, as the Owner of this little company, I am so proud of the **Quality People** I get to work with – both the **Teachers** and my **Team** – and the **Great Students** who get out and sell these books!

With much appreciation,

Grady W. Reed

Grady W. Reed, Owner
California Cookbook Company

P.S. See the re-order coupons on page 159.

Table of Contents

HOLIDAYS & PARTIES

On our front cover:
Covered with Kisses Chocolate Cherry Torte, page 78
Courtesy of Hershey Foods, Hershey, PA
and
Fiesta Dip, page 69
Courtesy of Lawry's Foods, Inc., Monrovia, CA

California Cookbook Company
ADVISORY COMMITTEE

KATHIE BACZYNSKI
Mt. Carmel High School, San Diego

PRISCELLA BURNS
Pleasant Valley High School, Chico

PAM CAMPION
Dublin High School, Dublin

CAROL DELAP
Golden West High School, Visalia

CINDY ELLEDGE
Johansen High School, Modesto

PEG ELLINGTON
Yucca Valley High School, Yucca Valley

PAM FECCHINO
Cimarron-Memorial HS, Las Vegas

PAM FORD
Temecula Valley High School, Temecula

MARIA FREGULIA
Lassen High School, Susanville

DEBBIE HARVEY
Amador Valley High School, Pleasanton

LaRAE HARGUESS
Hesperia High School, Hesperia

GERRY HENDERSON
Temple City High School, Temple City

GRACE HIBMA
Office of L.A. County Superintendent of Schools,
Consultant Consumer & Homemaking Education

CAMILLE HICKS
Riverton High School, Riverton

NANCY HUNYADI
Fullerton High School, Fullerton

REIKO IKKANDA
So. Pasadena Middle School, So. Pasadena

DOTTI JONES
Etiwanda High School, Etiwanda

MARY LASH
Paramount High School, Paramount

JERI LUNDY
Grossmont High School, La Mesa

JAN MARTIN
Spanish Springs High School, Sparks, NV

DORIS OITZMAN
Victor Valley High School, Victorville

ANN PORTER
San Luis Obispo High School, San Luis Obispo

BETTY RABIN
Sierra Vista Jr. High School, Canyon Country

APRIL ROSENDAHL
Chino High School, Chino

KAREN TILSON
Poly High School, Riverside

MARIANNE TRAW
Ball Junior High School, Anaheim

SONJA TYREE
Ayala High School, Chino Hills

BETTY WELLS
Bidwell Junior High School, Chico

KATHRYN P. WHITTEN
Home Economics Education, Fresno

Halloween

Deviled Mice

Serves: 6   *Appetizers & Beverages*

6 eggs
3 tablespoons Miracle Whip
1 teaspoon mustard
salt and pepper, to taste
2 sticks string cheese
2 olives

Place eggs in a medium saucepan with enough cold water to cover completely. Bring to a boil over medium heat and cook 12 minutes. Cool quickly with ice water so yolks stay yellow. Peel eggs and cut in half. Remove yolk and mash well with Miracle Whip, mustard, salt and pepper. Fill egg halves with yolk mixture and put halves back together. Cut a little off bottom of one half so they lay flat. Cut 1 stick string cheese into thin slices for the ears. Pull the other stick string cheese into long pieces for the tails. Slice olives and place just below ears for the eyes. Chill and serve.

"Fun to make with children."

Shauna Young   **Jordan High School, Sandy, UT**

Hot Lips

Serves: 4   *Appetizers & Beverages*

apples, Red Delicious, cut into wedges
lemon juice
peanut butter
miniature marshmallows

Dip apple slices into lemon juice (will prevent darkening). Spread peanut butter on one side of each slice. Top peanut butter with miniature marshmallows (to resemble teeth) and place apple slice on top of marshmallow, peanut butter side down. (It should resemble lips with teeth in middle). Secure with toothpicks. Enjoy!

Priscilla A. Robinson   **Mt. View High School, El Monte, CA**

Dinner In A Pumpkin

Serves: 8 - 10   *Beef Entreé*

2 pounds hamburger
6 ounces ham
$1/2$ onion, chopped
1 green pepper, chopped
2 teaspoons salt
$3/4$ teaspoon oregano
1 teaspoon vinegar
$1/2$ teaspoon garlic salt
$3/4$ teaspoon pepper
1 cup tomato sauce
1 (10") pumpkin, seeded, cleaned

Preheat oven to 350 degrees. Brown hamburger; drain grease. Add ham, onion and green pepper; cook until vegetables are tender. Add salt, oregano, vinegar, garlic salt, pepper and tomato sauce; mix well. Pour into pumpkin. Place pumpkin in shallow baking dish. Bake 1 hour.

"The presentation of this dish is fun!
Decorate side of pumpkin with a face and set on table."

Debi Spencer   **Colton High School, Colton, CA**

Halloween Cheese Beef Pies

Makes: 10   *Beef Entreé*

1 $1/2$ pounds ground beef
1 (medium) onion, chopped
1 tablespoon chili powder
dash salt
$1/2$ teaspoon garlic powder
1 (15 ounce) can tomato sauce
1 cup carrots, shredded
1 (4.5 ounce) can olives, chopped (optional)
1 (10 ounce) can refrigerated biscuits
10 slices American cheese

Brown beef and onion in a large skillet; pour off excess grease. Add seasonings. Stir in tomato sauce, carrots and olives. Cover and simmer 20 minutes, stirring occasionally. Preheat oven to 400 degrees. Roll each biscuit on floured board to make a 4" circle. Press each over greased bottom of muffin tin cups. Bake 10 minutes. Remove cups from tin immediately. Place cup-side up on baking sheet. Cut circles from cheese slices and make into pumpkin faces with a sharp knife. Put cheese scraps into meat mixture and stir until melted. Place meat mixture into biscuit cups. Top with cheese faces. Place in oven for 2 minutes more. Serve warm.

"These are especially fun with young children. As they get older, they
enjoy helping with the pumpkin faces and the preparation."

Barbara Henshaw   **Foothill High School, Pleasanton, CA**

Jack-O-Lantern Brownie

Serves: 12 -16   *Dessert*

   $3/4$ cup butter or margarine, melted
   1 $1/2$ cups sugar
   1 $1/2$ teaspoons vanilla
   3 eggs
   $3/4$ cup all-purpose flour
   $1/2$ cup Hershey's Cocoa
   $1/2$ teaspoon baking powder
   $1/4$ teaspoon salt
   yellow and red food color
   1 (16 ounce) can vanilla frosting
   Garnishes: Mini Kisses Baking Pieces; Twizzlers Nibs Licorice Bits;
      Twizzlers Pull 'n Peel; Skor or Heath English Toffee Bits

> *Photo opposite*
> *page 16*

Heat oven to 350 degrees. Grease 12" round pizza pan. (If using disposable pan, place on baking sheet to bake.) Beat melted butter, sugar and vanilla with spoon in large bowl. Beat in eggs. Stir in dry ingredients and beat with spoon until well blended. Spread into pan. Bake 20 to 22 minutes or until top springs back when touched lightly in center. Cool completely. Add yellow and red food color to frosting for desired shade of orange. Frost brownies. Garnish to resemble a jack-o-lantern.

Hershey Foods   **Hershey, PA**

Microwave Popcorn Balls

Makes: about 10 balls   *Dessert*

   $1/3$ cup light corn syrup
   $1/3$ cup water
   1 cup sugar
   1 teaspoon salt
   $1/4$ cup butter or margarine
   1 teaspoon vanilla
   food coloring (optional)
   7 to 9 cups popcorn, popped

Combine syrup, water, sugar, salt and margarine in buttered 4 cup glass measure. Cover with plastic wrap. Microwave on power level 7 for 2 minutes. Stir and continue cooking on power level 7 for 4 to 4 $1/2$ minutes. Stir and continue cooking at 4 minute intervals until candy forms a hard ball in cold water or reaches 250 degrees on candy thermometer. Stir in vanilla and food coloring, being careful of steam when you add the liquid to the syrup. Pour in thin stream over popped popcorn in a large buttered bowl. Mix well. Butter hands; lightly sprinkle with water and shape into 2 $1/2$" balls. Wrap each ball in plastic wrap.

Rene Crepaldi   **Reed High School, Sparks, NV**

Pumpkin Crunch Cake

Serves: 9 - 12   *Dessert*

1 (1 pound 13 ounce) can pumpkin
3 eggs, beaten
1 can evaporated milk
$3/4$ cup sugar
1 teaspoon cinnamon
1 box yellow cake mix
1 cup walnuts, chopped
$1/2$ cup butter, melted
1 (8 ounce) package cream cheese, softened
$1/2$ cup powdered sugar
$3/4$ cup Cool Whip

Preheat oven to 350 degrees. Line a 9" x 13" pan with waxed paper. In a
large bowl, mix pumpkin, eggs, milk, sugar and cinnamon until well
blended. Pour into pan over waxed paper. Sprinkle box of cake mix over
top. Pat walnuts over cake, then spoon melted butter over all. Bake 50 to 60
minutes; cool. Combine cream cheese with powdered sugar and beat until
smooth. Fold in Cool Whip. After cake has cooled, turn out onto serving
dish and remove waxed paper. Frost with cream cheese frosting and
refrigerate. Serve chilled.

"I make this every year for my students on Halloween for a treat.
Great as a pumpkin pie substitute."

Julie Eyre   **Alhambra High School, Alhambra, CA**

Pumpkin Ice Cream Pie

Serves: 6 - 8   *Dessert*

$1/2$ cup vanilla ice cream
1 cup canned pumpkin
$1/2$ cup brown sugar
$1/4$ teaspoon cinnamon
$1/2$ teaspoon ginger
$1/4$ teaspoon nutmeg
1 tablespoon orange juice
9" prepared graham cracker crust
Whipped cream

Scoop ice cream into a bowl and allow to soften. In a second bowl, blend
pumpkin, sugar, spices and orange juice with an electric mixer. Fold into
softened ice cream. Spoon into graham cracker crust. Freeze. Let pie sit out
10 to 15 minutes before serving. Garnish with whipped cream.

"A refreshing holiday dessert!"

Nanci Burkhart   **Hueneme High School, Oxnard, CA**

Pumpkin Pie Squares

Serves: 8 - 10   *Dessert*

  1 (13 ounce) can evaporated milk
  1 (large) can pumpkin
  3 eggs
  1 $1/2$ teaspoons cinnamon
  $1/2$ teaspoon nutmeg
  $1/4$ teaspoon allspice
  1 cup sugar
  $1/2$ teaspoon salt
  1 box yellow cake mix
  1 $1/2$ cubes butter or margarine
  $1/2$ to 1 cup nuts, chopped

Preheat oven to 350 degrees. Combine first 8 ingredients; mix well. Pour into a greased 9" x 13" pan. Sprinkle cake mix over top of mixture. Slice butter and dot over cake mix. Sprinkle with nuts. Bake 50 minutes, or until set in center.

"This is very tasty and a good alternative to pumpkin pie."

Pamela Buldo-McGowen   **Redwood High School, Visalia, CA**

Pumpkin Roll

Makes: 2 logs   *Dessert*

  3 eggs
  1 cup sugar
  $2/3$ cup pumpkin
  1 teaspoon baking soda
  $1/2$ teaspoon salt
  1 teaspoon cinnamon
  $3/4$ cup flour
  8 ounces cream cheese
  1 teaspoon vanilla
  2 tablespoons butter or margarine
  1 cup powdered sugar

Preheat oven to 375 degrees. Line a large cookie sheet (or jelly roll pan with $1/2$" sides) with waxed paper. Beat together eggs, sugar and pumpkin for 5 minutes. Add baking soda, salt, cinnamon, and flour; mix well. Spread batter onto waxed paper with spatula. Bake 15 minutes. Let stand 5 minutes, then quickly cut in half and roll up, along with waxed paper and place in refrigerator. While it cools, combine cream cheese with vanilla, butter or margarine and powdered sugar. Remove roll from refrigerator, remove waxed paper and unroll. Spread frosting over cake and roll up again. To keep tight, wrap in clear plastic wrap. For best results, freeze so that log is hard when you cut it.

Holly Tessier   **West High School, Torrance, CA**

Pumpkin Walnut Cookies

Makes: 15   *Dessert*

$1/4$ cup butter or margarine
$3/4$ cup brown sugar, packed
1 egg
$1/2$ cup canned pumpkin
$1/2$ teaspoon vanilla
$1/2$ teaspoon lemon peel, grated
$1/2$ teaspoon lemon juice
1 $1/4$ cups flour, sifted
1 $1/2$ teaspoons baking powder
$1/2$ teaspoon salt
$3/4$ teaspoon pumpkin pie spice
$1/8$ teaspoon ginger
$1/2$ cup walnuts, coarsely chopped
Butter Frosting:
6 tablespoons butter, softened
1 (1 pound) package confectioner's sugar (about 4 cups)
$1/4$ cup cream
1 $1/2$ teaspoons vanilla

Preheat oven to 375 degrees. Cream butter and sugar until fluffy. Beat in egg. Stir in pumpkin, vanilla, lemon peel and lemon juice. Sift flour again with baking powder, salt and spices. Blend into creamed mixture. Stir in walnuts. Drop by tablespoonfuls onto greased baking sheet. Bake 12 to 14 minutes.

Butter Frosting: Cream butter. Gradually add about half the confectioner's sugar. Beat in 2 tablespoons cream and vanilla. Gradually blend in remaining sugar. Add enough cream to make spreading consistency. (This will frost a layer cake or 2 to 3 batches of pumpkin cookies).

Sheron Owens & Shelly Tresley   **McQueen High School, Reno, NV**

Thanksgiving

Holiday Wassail

Serves: 18 - 20   *Appetizers & Beverages*

1 gallon apple juice
1 (46 ounce) bottle apricot nectar
1 teaspoon dried chunk orange peel (about $1/2''$ in size)
1 teaspoon whole cloves
1 teaspoon cinnamon sticks, broken up
$1/2$ teaspoon whole allspice

In a large stock pot, bring juice and nectar to a boil. In a simmering cheesecloth bag, combine orange peel with cloves, cinnamon stick pieces and allspice. Add spice bag to juice mixture and secure string to the handle of stock pot. Bring to a boil, then reduce heat to simmer. Cook about 20 minutes. Check the flavor of wassail, if it's not strong enough, let spices simmer until desired flavor has been achieved. Note: Purchase a package of "Mulling Spices" at a kitchen store and use in place of spices in cheesecloth.

"I serve this recipe from the onset of fall, through Christmas.
It is one of my family's favorite recipes."
Christine Katsilas   Taylorsville High School, Taylorsville, UT

Buttermilk Biscuits

Makes: 12   *Breads/Baked Goods*

1 $3/4$ cups all-purpose flour
1 teaspoon salt
2 teaspoons double acting baking powder
1 teaspoon sugar
$1/2$ teaspoon baking soda
5 tablespoons butter
$2/3$ to $3/4$ cup buttermilk

Preheat oven to 450 degrees. Mix dry ingredients. Cut in butter. Add enough buttermilk so the dough holds together. Do not overstir. Drop by the spoonful onto cookie sheets or baking stones. Bake 10 to 12 minutes.

"This recipe was given to me by the owners of Huasna Valley Organic
Farm. They are my family's favorite at Thanksgiving!"
Val Poalillo   Paso Robles High School, Paso Robles, CA

Pumpkin Bread

Makes: 3 loaves   *Breads/Baked Goods*

2 1/2 cups flour
3 cups sugar
2 teaspoons baking soda
2 teaspoons pumpkin pie spice
2 teaspoons cinnamon
2 teaspoons nutmeg
1 1/2 teaspoons salt
4 eggs
1/2 cup + 3 tablespoons water
1 cup oil
2 cups canned pumpkin
1/2 cup nuts, chopped

Preheat oven to 350 degrees. Prepare 3 loaf pans with nonstick cooking spray. Combine all ingredients and pour into prepared pans. Bake 1 hour.

"I prepare these for family, friends and neighbors at Thanksgiving time. A quick recipe, and everyone loves the bread because it's so moist!"

Teresa Watson   **Don Juan Avila Middle School, Aliso Viejo, CA**

Pumpkin Donuts

Makes: 2 dozen   *Breads/Baked Goods*

2 tablespoons shortening
3/4 cup sugar
2 eggs
1 cup pumpkin
1 cup shredded bran cereal
2 3/4 cups flour
2 teaspoons baking powder
1 teaspoon pumpkin pie spice
1/2 teaspoon salt
Topping: 4 tablespoons sugar mixed with 3 teaspoons cinnamon
oil, for deep frying

Beat shortening and sugar in large bowl until fluffy. Beat in eggs one at a time. Stir in pumpkin, then cereal. Let stand 2 minutes. Sift together flour, baking powder, pumpkin pie spice and salt. Stir into pumpkin mixture, half at a time. Cover and chill at least 1 hour. Combine topping and set aside. Roll chilled dough to 1/2" thick. Cut into rounds and balls with 3" cutter. In a fry pan, heat oil to 375 degrees. Fry donuts until golden brown, approximately 2 minutes on each side. Remove from oil and drain on paper towels. While still warm, sprinkle with cinnamon/sugar mixture.

"Our boys' favorite Thanksgiving morning treat, and they cook!"

Chrisann Boone   **Reedley High School, Reedley, CA**

Cranberry Chutney

Makes: 6 cups   *Salad*

- 1 cup pecans
- 12 ounces fresh cranberries
- 2 Granny Smith apples, cored, chopped
- 2 oranges, zested and juiced
- 1 $1/2$ cups light brown sugar
- $3/4$ cup water
- $2/3$ cup apple cider vinegar
- 1 (medium) onion
- $1/2$ cup dried apricot halves, coarsely chopped
- 1 tablespoon crystallized ginger, chopped
- $1/2$ teaspoon hot pepper flakes
- nutmeg, freshly grated

Preheat oven to 350 degrees. Spread pecans in a single layer on small baking sheet. Bake until golden and aromatic, 8 to 12 minutes. Shake pan halfway though baking to make sure nuts toast evenly. Cool and coarsely chop; set aside. Combine cranberries, apples, orange zest and juice, sugar, water, vinegar, onion, apricots, ginger, pepper flakes and nutmeg in large saucepan. Place over medium heat and cook, stirring frequently, for 30 minutes. Stir in pecans. Cool to room temperature and serve, or store refrigerated in airtight container for up to 1 week.

"Makes a wonderful alternative to canned cranberry sauce."

Donna Fippen   **Bret Harte High School, Altaville, CA**

Cranberry Jello

Serves: 18 - 20   *Salad*

- 2 (3 ounce) packages cherry jello
- 2 cups boiling water
- 1 package Knox gelatin
- $1/2$ cup cold water
- 2 cans whole cranberry sauce
- 1 (16 ounce) carton sour cream

Dissolve jello in boiling water; set aside. Soften Knox gelatin in cold water. Stir gelatin into jello mixture and place in refrigerator until firm. Remove from refrigerator and stir in cranberry sauce. Add sour cream. Place in large bowl; cover until ready to serve.

"Our Thanksgiving meal isn't complete unless we have cranberry jello!"

Astrid Curfman   **Newcomb Academy, Long Beach, CA**

Cranberry Salad

Serves: 6 - 8   *Salad*

2 cups fresh cranberries, ground
3 cups miniature marshmallows
$^3/_4$ cup sugar
2 cups tart apples, unpeeled, diced
$^1/_2$ cup seedless green grapes
$^1/_2$ cup walnuts, chopped
1 cup whipping cream, whipped OR 2 cups whipped topping

Combine cranberries, marshmallows and sugar; chill overnight. Next day, stir in apples, grapes and nuts. Fold in whipping cream or topping. Chill several hours.

"Delicious with ham or turkey!"

Doris Oitzman   **Victor Valley High School, Victorville, CA**

Cranberry Whip

Serves: 8 - 10   *Salad*

1 package fresh cranberries
1 cup sugar
1 cup pineapple tidbits
$^1/_2$ bag miniature marshmallows
1 cup whipping cream

Wash cranberries and chop until very fine in food processor. Place in bowl; add sugar and refrigerate 2 hours. Toss in pineapple and marshmallows and refrigerate overnight. Just before serving, fold in whipped cream.

"The only way mother could get me to eat cranberries at Thanksgiving!"

Michelle Miller   **Aliso Viejo Middle School, Aliso Viejo, CA**

Denise's Pomegranate Jello

Serves: 10 - 12   *Salad*

3 (small) packages raspberry jello
3 cups water
1 (No. 2) can crushed pineapple
1 (16 ounce) package frozen raspberries
1 can whole cranberry sauce
2 cups pomegranate seeds

Prepare raspberry jello using only 3 cups boiling water to dissolve. Add remaining ingredients to jello and pour into bundt pan. Chill until set.

"This is a beautiful rich red dish that is very festive with turkey or ham."

Anne Silveira   **Shasta High School, Redding, CA**

Frosted Salad

Serves: 12   *Salad*

2 (3 ounce) packages lemon jello
2 cups boiling water
2 cups 7-Up
1 (20 ounce) can crushed pineapple, drained, reserved
1 cup miniature marshmallows
2 (large) bananas
Topping:
$1/2$ cup sugar
2 tablespoons flour
1 cup reserved pineapple juice (from canned crushed pineapple)
1 egg
2 tablespoons butter or margarine
$1/4$ cup Velveeta cheese, cubed
$1/2$ of a half-pint heavy whipping cream
3 tablespoons Parmesan cheese, grated

Combine first three ingredients and allow to set partially. Add next three ingredients, being certain to drain and reserve juice from pineapple and pour into a 9" x 13" glass dish. Prepare topping: In saucepan, mix sugar and flour; stir in reserved pineapple juice, adding water if necessary to make 1 cup. Add egg and cook over low heat, stirring constantly until thick; remove from heat. Stir in butter and Velveeta; blend. Chill. Whip whipping cream and fold into chilled topping. Spread over jello and sprinkle with Parmesan cheese.

> *"Be sure to cook the topping ingredients over a very low flame and stir, stir, stir. Your family will love this salad!"*

Karen Gray   Mira Mesa High School, San Diego, CA

Baked Spiced Butternut Squash with Apples & Maple Syrup

Serves: 10 - 12   *Vegetable/Side Dish*

$1/2$ cup butter
$3/4$ cup pure maple syrup
$1/4$ cup apple juice
1 teaspoon ground cinnamon
$1/2$ teaspoon ground allspice
$1/2$ teaspoon salt
$1/4$ teaspoon freshly ground pepper
3 pounds butternut squash, peeled, halved lengthwise,
    seeded, cut crosswise into $1/3$" thick slices
4 (6 ounce) Granny Smith apples, peeled, halved, cored,
    cut into $1/4$" thick slices

Butter a 9" x 13" glass baking dish. Stir butter, maple syrup and apple juice in a small saucepan over medium-low heat until butter melts. Increase heat and boil until mixture is slightly reduced; about 5 minutes. Remove from heat and whisk in cinnamon, allspice and salt. Arrange squash and apple slices in rows, alternating them, in prepared dish. Sprinkle lightly with salt and pepper. Pour maple syrup mixture over all. Cover dish tightly with foil. Bake until squash is almost tender, about 50 minutes. Uncover and bake until squash is tender, basting occasionally with syrup, about 20 minutes longer. Spoon syrup from dish over squash and apples and serve. Note: Can be made 1 day ahead and warmed in a 350 degree oven for 25 minutes or microwave on HIGH for about 10 minutes.

Kathy Ewing   **Johansen High School, Modesto, CA**

Carrot Puff

Serves: 4   *Vegetable/Side Dish*

    1 pound (4 medium) carrots, peeled, cut in half
    3 tablespoons flour
    1 teaspoon vanilla
    3 eggs
    dash nutmeg
    $1/8$ teaspoon cayenne
    $1/4$ teaspoon curry powder
    $1/3$ cup butter, melted
    $1/4$ cup pecans, coarsely chopped

Preheat oven to 350 degrees. Cook carrots in boiling water until tender; drain and cool in ice water; drain again. Place cooled carrots, flour, vanilla, eggs, nutmeg, cayenne, curry powder and melted (but not hot) butter in blender. Puree in blender until completely smooth, scraping sides if needed. Pour into a 1 quart baking or souffle dish. Bake in oven 40 minutes. Sprinkle on pecans and bake an additional 10 minutes. Serve immediately.

"Unusual and simple - a great show off piece.
Tastes great and a different way to prepare carrots!"

Pam Bonilla   **Valley View High School, Moreno Valley, CA**

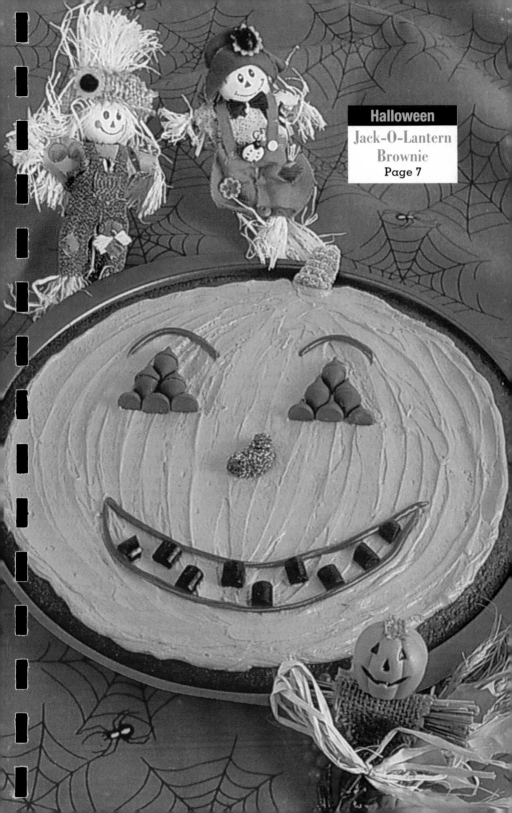

Halloween
Jack-O-Lantern
Brownie
Page 7

Hanukkah

Hanukkah
Dreidel Brownies
Page 30

Crusty Sweet Potato Pie

Serves: 12　　　　　　　　　　　　　***Vegetable/Side Dish***

1 (large) can yams
$1/2$ cup sugar
2 eggs
$1/4$ cup butter
1 teaspoon vanilla
$1/3$ cup milk
Topping:
$1/3$ cup butter
$1/3$ cup brown sugar
$1/2$ cup oatmeal
1 cup pecans, chopped

Preheat oven to 350 degrees. Spray a 9" x 13" casserole with non stick cooking spray. Combine yams with sugar, eggs, butter, vanilla and milk; mix with electric mixer. Pour into casserole dish and bake 20 minutes. Meanwhile, combine topping ingredients. Remove yams from oven and sprinkle with topping. Bake 5 minutes more.

"A family favorite for the holidays!"

Tracie Priske　　　　　　　　　**Valencia High School, Valencia, CA**

Easy Berry Relish

Makes: 5 cups　　　　　　　　***Vegetable/Side Dish***

1 (12 ounce) package fresh cranberries
2 $1/2$ cups sugar
1 $2/3$ cups ginger ale
$1/3$ cup lemon juice
1 (3 ounce) package raspberry gelatin

In a saucepan, combine first four ingredients. Cook over medium heat until berries pop, about 15 minutes. Remove from heat and stir in gelatin until dissolved. Pour into serving bowl. Chill overnight.

"Found this in Taste Of Home, *I make it every year. Such great flavor!"*

Monica Blanchette　　　　　**Landmark Middle School, Moreno Valley, CA**

Mashed Potato Casserole

Serves: 8 - 12　　　　　　　　***Vegetable/Side Dish***

6 pounds potatoes
4 to 6 cloves garlic, peeled
8 ounces cream cheese
1 cup sour cream
$1/4$ to $1/2$ cup butter
salt and pepper, to taste

Peel and boil potatoes with garlic until tender; drain and mash until all lumps are gone. Stir in cream cheese, sour cream and butter until smooth. Add salt and pepper to taste. Place in a 9" x 13" casserole dish. (At this point, the casserole may be covered with foil and refrigerated until next day.) Bake, uncovered, at 350 degrees for 1 hour, or until thoroughly heated.

"A wonderful recipe to save last minute preparations on holidays."
Liz Aschenbrenner   Sierra High School, Manteca, CA

Nutty Cranberries
Serves: 6   *Vegetable/Side Dish*
 2 cans whole cranberries
 1 can spiced peaches
 1/4 cup walnuts, chopped

Combine all ingredients in saucepan; bring to a boil. Turn down heat and simmer 1 hour. Cool. Refrigerate until firm.

Jane Souza   North Monterey County High School, Castroville, CA

Sage Stuffing
Serves: 12 - 16   *Vegetable/Side Dish*
 2 loaves heavy white bread
 3 (large) onions
 4 1/2 cups water, divided
 1/2 cup ground sage
 1 pound butter
 1 teaspoon pepper
 1/2 teaspoon poultry seasoning
 1/4 teaspoon celery salt
 1 pinch rosemary
 2 tablespoons salt

Cut bread into cubes and let dry out overnight. In a blender, combine onions, 1 1/2 cups water and sage until ground up; set aside. In a large pot, melt butter. Add blender ingredients, pepper, poultry seasoning, celery salt, rosemary, salt and remaining 3 cups water. Bring to a boil and simmer 30 minutes. Cool 20 minutes. Pour over dry bread crumbs and stuff bird. Wrap any leftover stuffing in foil and cook with turkey in the last hour of cooking time.

"My dad made this stuffing as far back as I can remember. He's passed this to his children and grandchildren and, I hope, beyond that!"
Laurie deJong   Bingham High School, So. Jordan, UT

Sausage, Apple & Chestnut Stuffing

Makes: 12 cups   *Vegetable/Side Dish*

1 pound country-style white bread, crust trimmed, cut into $1/2$" cubes
$3/4$ pound bulk pork sausage
4 tablespoons butter
1 (large) yellow onion, chopped
3 (large) celery stalks, chopped
2 (large) tart apples, peeled, quartered, chopped
3 tablespoons fresh thyme, chopped OR 1 tablespoon dried thyme
$3/4$ cup chicken broth
1 pound fresh chestnuts, baked, peeled,
    OR 2 cups vacuum-packed chestnuts, peeled
$1/2$ cup fresh parsley, chopped
salt and freshly ground pepper, to taste
2 eggs, well beaten

Preheat oven to 400 degrees. Place bread cubes in a large baking pan. Bake, stirring occasionally, until lightly golden, about 12 minutes. Transfer to a large bowl. In large frying pan over medium-high heat, cook sausage, crumbling with a fork, until browned, about 10 minutes. Transfer to bowl with bread. Add butter to sausage drippings in frying pan, reduce heat to medium and melt butter. Add onion and celery and saute until tender, about 8 minutes. Add apples, and thyme; saute 1 $1/2$ minutes. Add to bread/sausage mixture. Add broth to the pan and bring to a boil, scraping any browned bits. Add to the bread/sausage mixture. Mix in chestnuts and parsley and season with salt and pepper. Mix in eggs.
To stuff a turkey: Fill the large body cavity and smaller neck cavity with stuffing. Bake any remaining stuffing per instructions below.
To bake: Preheat oven to 325 degrees. Butter a 12" x 9" x 2" baking dish and spoon the stuffing into it. Cover with foil and bake 30 minutes; uncover and bake until top is crisp, about 30 minutes longer.
Kathie Baczynski   **Mt. Carmel High School, Poway, CA**

Sweet Potato Balls

Makes: 8 - 10   *Vegetable/Side Dish*

2 $1/2$ cups sweet potatoes, baked, mashed
$1/2$ teaspoon salt
dash pepper
3 tablespoons butter, divided
10 marshmallows
$1/3$ cup honey
1 cup pecans, chopped

Combine sweet potatoes, salt, pepper and 2 tablespoons melted butter; chill. Preheat oven to 350 degrees. Shape potatoes into 2" balls with a marshmallow inside each. Use $1/4$ cup mashed potato to cover. Heat honey and remaining 1 tablespoon butter in pan. When hot, roll balls with fork in glaze to coat completely, Roll in nuts and bake 20 to 25 minutes.

"This yummy recipe was given to me by former student, Lara Mendizza."

Rhonda Nelson   **Rancho Santa Margarita Intermediate School, RSM, CA**

Sweet Potato Casserole

Serves: 10 - 12   *Vegetable/Side Dish*

1 (40 ounce) can sweet potatoes, drained
1 cup sugar
2 eggs
$2/3$ cup butter, melted, divided
$1/3$ cup milk
1 cup brown sugar, firmly packed
1 cup pecans, chopped
$1/3$ cup flour

Preheat oven to 350 degrees. Grease a 2 quart baking dish. Combine sweet potatoes, sugar, eggs, $1/3$ cup melted butter, and milk in large mixing bowl with electric mixer until well combined. Place in prepared baking dish. In a small bowl combine brown sugar, pecans, flour and remaining $1/3$ cup butter. Sprinkle over top of sweet potato mixture. Bake 35 minutes or until knife inserted in center comes out clean.

"Sweet potatoes were not a big favorite until my mom found this recipe. Now, it wouldn't be Thanksgiving without it!"

Renee Fertig   **No. Monterey Co. High School, Castroville, CA**

Sweet Potato Puffs

Serves: 6   *Vegetable/Side Dish*

5 sweet potatoes
4 egg whites
1 $1/4$ cups sugar
1 teaspoon vanilla
5 tablespoons flour, divided
Topping:
$1/2$ cup brown sugar
2 tablespoons butter, softened
$1/2$ cup pecans, chopped

Gently boil sweet potatoes in skins; cool, remove skins and slice into tidbits. Preheat oven to 350 degrees. In a mixer or food processor, blend sweet potatoes with egg whites, 1 $1/4$ cups sugar, vanilla and 2 tablespoons flour. Transfer to a 1 $1/4$ quart casserole dish that has been sprayed with nonstick cooking spray. Using fingers, blend brown sugar with remaining 3 tablespoons flour and butter. Stir in pecans and sprinkle over casserole. Bake 20 to 30 minutes.

"A Thanksgiving delight. Thanks to my friend, Reed, for this recipe."

Ruth Anne Mills   **Los Alisos Intermediate School, Mission Viejo, CA**

Sweet Potato Soufflé

Serves: 8   *Vegetable/Side Dish*

3 pounds sweet potatoes, raw OR 2 pounds, cooked, peeled, mashed
$3/4$ cup sugar
$3/4$ cup orange juice
$1/2$ teaspoon salt
1 egg, beaten
3 tablespoons butter
1 teaspoon vanilla
$1/4$ cup coconut (optional)
marshmallows (optional)

Preheat oven to 350 degrees. Place sweet potatoes in large pan and cover with water. Bring to a boil. Boil until fork tender. While sweet potatoes are hot, peel and mash. Add remaining ingredients, except optional items, and mix well. (If mixture seems dry, add more orange juice.) Pour into 1 $1/2$ quart casserole. Bake 30 minutes. Top with coconut and marshmallow and return to oven until browned.

*"This is a Thanksgiving favorite! My college students
are calling for this recipe. A family standard."*

Jan Tuttle   **Mills High School, Millbrae, CA**

Zippy Cranberry Relish

Serves: 6 - 8   *Vegetable/Side Dish*

1 pound fresh cranberries
1 (12 ounce) can crushed pineapple, drained
$1/3$ cup orange peel, grated
$1/2$ teaspoon ground cinnamon
$1/2$ teaspoon powdered ginger
1 ounce sweet vermouth

Prepare cranberries according to package directions for whole cranberry sauce. Add drained pineapple, orange peel, cinnamon, ginger and sweet vermouth. Chill at least 24 hours.

Mary Coffman   **Reed High School, Sparks, NV**

After Thanksgiving Casserole

Serves: 6 - 8   *Chicken Entreé*

2 (5 ounce) cans boned chicken or turkey, OR equal amount leftovers
1 (10.5 ounce) can condensed cream of chicken soup
1 (6 serving size) package chicken flavor stuffing mix
3 cups mashed potatoes, prepared

Combine poultry with soup; set aside. Prepare stuffing mix on top of range or in microwave according to package directions; place in baking dish. Spread mashed potatoes over stuffing. Top with soup mixture and cook in microwave on HIGH 5 minutes or bake in preheated 350 degree oven for 20 minutes.

"Can be made and frozen for later. Great for using up those Thanksgiving leftovers. It is quick and easy to make. You will have the warm thoughts of Thanksgiving by eating this anytime throughout the year."

Laurie Giauque   **Olympus High School, Salt Lake City, UT**

Leftover Turkey Enchiladas

Serves: 12   *Chicken Entreé*

        2 tablespoon oil
        1 (medium) onion, chopped
        1 clove garlic, minced
        2 cups turkey, cooked, shredded
        2 cups cheddar cheese, shredded, divided
        2 cups Monterey jack cheese, shredded, divided
        4 tablespoons shortening
        4 tablespoons flour
        3 tablespoons chili powder
        dash cumin powder
        1 teaspoon salt
        2 cups chicken broth
        12 flour tortillas

Heat oil in frying pan and saute onion and garlic. Remove from heat and add turkey, 1 cup cheddar cheese and 1 cup jack cheese; mix well and set aside. Prepare sauce: Melt shortening in medium saucepan over medium heat. Whisk in flour, chili powder, cumin and salt to make a roux. Slowly stir in chicken broth and cook until sauce thickens. Preheat oven to 350 degrees. Assemble enchiladas: Warm tortillas, a few at a time, in microwave on HIGH for 1 minute. Put tortilla on a plate and spoon $1/4$ cup turkey filling in the middle of each tortilla. Roll up and place seam side down in a 9" x 13" lightly greased pan. Repeat with remaining tortillas and filling. Spoon sauce over enchiladas and top with remaining cheese. Bake 30 minutes, until hot and bubbly.

"A delicious way to use up leftover turkey from Thanksgiving and Christmas! The homemade sauce adds great flavor!"

Beth Cropsey Guerrero   **Selma High School, Selma, CA**

Stackie Uppie

Serves: Lots   *Chicken Entreé*

rice, cooked
chow mein noodles
turkey, sliced
tomatoes, chopped
pineapple chunks
onion, diced
gravy
peanuts or cashews
coconut, shredded

Put all ingredients in separate bowls and platters. Let guests stack up desired foods and top with gravy, nuts and coconut. Serve with warm crescents or rolls.

"Great with leftover turkey from Thanksgiving.
This is an easy meal to serve to large groups."

Linda Olsen   **Folsom High School, Folsom, CA**

Thanksgiving Pot Pie

Serves: 4 - 6   *Chicken Entreé*

2 pie crusts
$1/4$ cup margarine
$3/4$ cup celery, chopped
1 (small) onion, minced
3 tablespoons flour
1 teaspoon dried parsley flakes
$1/2$ teaspoon dried thyme
salt and pepper, to taste
$1/3$ cup milk
$1/2$ cup chicken broth
2 cups turkey, cut into small cubes
1 package frozen mixed vegetables

Line a deep dish pie plate with one pie crust. Preheat oven to 425 degrees. In large skillet, melt margarine. Saute celery and onion until soft; stir in flour to thicken. Add seasonings. Stir in milk and broth slowly to make a medium cream sauce. Add turkey and mixed vegetables. Cool slightly and pour into pie crust. Form second crust on top; flute edges to seal. Cut a vent in top center and bake 30 minutes.

"A family and class favorite!"

Gail McAuley   **Lincoln High School, Stockton, CA**

Aunt Julie's Pumpkin Pie

Serves: 6 - 8   *Dessert*

2 $1/2$ cups pumpkin
$1/4$ cup cream
2 eggs, well beaten
1 cup sugar
1 tablespoon flour
1 teaspoon salt
$1/4$ teaspoon cinnamon
$1/4$ teaspoon nutmeg
$1/4$ teaspoon allspice
$1/2$ teaspoon lemon extract
$1/2$ teaspoon vanilla
1 $1/2$ tablespoons butter, melted
1 pastry pie crust, prepared
1 cup pecans
$1/4$ cup margarine
1 cup brown sugar
whipped cream

Preheat oven to 450 degrees. Mix together pumpkin, cream and eggs. Stir in sugar, flour, salt, spices, lemon extract, vanilla and melted butter. Pour into prepared pie crust. Bake at 450 degrees for 15 minutes, then lower temperature to 325 and bake 30 minutes more, or until knife inserted in center comes out clean. While pie bakes, combine pecans with margarine and brown sugar. Remove baked pie from oven and cover with pecan topping. Place under broiler until topping is caramelized. Watch carefully so it doesn't burn. Serve warm with whipped cream.

"One of our family's favorite Thanksgiving recipes from my Great Aunt Julia Rugg, also a Home Economics teacher at Chaffey High School."

Deborah Scott-Toux   **Eisenhower High School, Rialto, CA**

Glenn's Pumpkin Pie Crunch

Serves: 12   *Dessert*

1 (16 ounce) can pumpkin
1 (12 ounce) can evaporated milk
3 eggs
1 $1/2$ cups sugar
4 teaspoons pumpkin pie spice
$1/2$ teaspoon salt
1 yellow cake mix
1 cup butter, melted
1 cup pecans, chopped

Preheat oven to 350 degrees. Combine pumpkin, milk, eggs, sugar, spice and salt in a bowl. Pour into a buttered 9" x 13" glass baking dish. Sprinkle cake mix evenly over pumpkin mixture and drizzle with melted butter. Top with pecans. Bake 50 to 55 minutes. Top with whipped topping.

"Great change at Thanksgiving from the traditional pumpkin pie.
A family favorite from Glenn Killingsworth - Chaffey High School."

Sonja Tyree   Ayala High School, Chino, CA

Pumpkin Cheesecake

Serves: 10   *Dessert*

butter
$1/4$ cup graham cracker crumbs
4 (8 ounce) packages cream cheese, softened
1 $1/2$ cups sugar
5 (large) eggs
$1/4$ cup flour
$1/4$ teaspoon salt
1 (1 pound) can pumpkin
2 teaspoons pumpkin pie spice
$1/2$ cup heavy cream, whipped

Generously butter bottom and sides of a 9" springform pan. Sprinkle with cracker crumbs, shaking pan to coat all sides. Let excess crumbs remain on bottom. Heat oven to 325 degrees. Beat cream cheese in large bowl until fluffy. Beat in sugar gradually. Add eggs, one at a time, beating well after each addition. Beat in flour, salt, pumpkin and spice. Pour into prepared pan. Bake 1 hour, 30 minutes or until firm around sides but soft in center. Turn off heat. (Top of cake will have cracked during baking.) Open oven door and let cake cool in oven. Cool completely on wire rack. Remove sides of pan. Chill cake and garnish with whipped cream.

"One-half recipe can be made in a 9" pie pan and cooked for 1 hour.
Can also be wrapped in foil and frozen.
Thaw, uncovered, in refrigerator before serving."

Sue Hope   Lompoc High School, Lompoc, CA

Pumpkin Crunch Dessert

Serves: 8 - 12   *Dessert*

1 (large) can pumpkin
3 eggs
1 (large) can evaporated milk
1 cup sugar
4 teaspoons pumpkin pie spice
1 box yellow cake mix
2 cubes margarine, melted

Preheat oven to 350 degrees. Blend together pumpkin, eggs, milk, sugar and spice. Pour into a 9" x 13" cake pan. Sprinkle dry cake mix over top, covering completely. Drizzle melted butter over top of dry mix. Bake 45 to 50 minutes. Serve warm or cooled with whipped cream.

"According to my family, it's better than a pumpkin pie...easier too!"
Jeanette Neese   **Enterprise High School, Redding, CA**

Pumpkin Delight

Serves: 8   *Dessert*

    4 eggs, lightly beaten
    1 (large) can pumpkin
    1 $1/2$ cups sugar
    1 teaspoon salt
    1 teaspoon pumpkin pie spice
    1 (12 ounce) can evaporated milk
    1 package yellow cake mix
    1 cup butter, melted
    1 cup nuts, chopped

Preheat oven to 350 degrees (325 degrees if using glass pan). Blend eggs with pumpkin. Add sugar, salt and spice; blend well. Add milk and blend. Pour batter into 9" x 13" ungreased pan. Sprinkle cake mix on top. Spoon on melted butter, then sprinkle with nuts. Bake 1 $1/4$ hours.

"Given to me by Karen Griffin, a teacher at Valley View. When Karen brings this dessert to a potluck, she gets many requests for the recipe."
Cheri Schuette   **Valley View Middle School, Simi Valley, CA**

Pumpkin Dessert Cake

Serves: 12   *Dessert*

    Crust:
    1 package yellow cake mix, divided
    1 egg, beaten
    $1/2$ cup margarine, melted
    Filling:
    1 (30 ounce) can pumpkin
    $3/4$ cup brown sugar
    2 eggs
    1 $1/2$ teaspoons nutmeg
    $1/2$ teaspoon salt
    $2/3$ cup evaporated milk
    Topping:
    $1/4$ cup sugar
    $1/4$ cup margarine, softened

Preheat oven to 350 degrees. Grease and flour a 9" x 13" pan. Put cake mix in medium mixing bowl and measure 1 cup cake mix; remove and set aside for topping. Beat egg and add to cake mix along with melted butter; mix well. Press mixture into pan. Using an electric mixer, thoroughly mix all the filling ingredients; pour over crust. In a small bowl, combine topping ingredients with reserved 1 cup cake mix; mix with hands until crumbled. Sprinkle mixture over top of filling. Bake 50 minutes.

"A good substitute for pumpkin pie, and it serves more!"

Connie Halloway   Rubidoux High School, Riverside, CA

Pumpkin Roll

Makes: 1 log   *Dessert*

- 3 eggs
- 1 cup sugar
- $2/3$ cup pumpkin
- 1 teaspoon lemon juice
- $3/4$ cup flour
- 1 teaspoon baking powder
- 1 teaspoon cinnamon
- 1 teaspoon ginger
- $1/2$ teaspoon nutmeg
- $1/2$ teaspoon salt
- $1/2$ cup walnuts (optional)
- 1 cup powdered sugar
- 8 ounce cream cheese
- 4 tablespoons butter
- $1/2$ teaspoon vanilla

Preheat oven to 375 degrees. Beat eggs 3 to 4 minutes. Gradually add sugar, pumpkin and lemon juice. Fold in flour, baking powder, cinnamon, ginger, nutmeg, salt and walnuts. Pour into a greased and floured jelly roll pan. Bake 10 to 15 minutes. Let rest 3 minutes. Turn out onto towel that has been sprinkled with powdered sugar; roll up. Meanwhile, mix together 1 cup powdered sugar, cream cheese butter and vanilla. Unroll pumpkin roll and frost with filling; roll up again. Wrap in plastic wrap and freeze for 6 hours.

Celeste Giron   Riverton High School, Riverton, UT

Pumpkin Trifle

Serves: 12 - 15   *Dessert*

3 cups leftover unfrosted spice cake, muffins or gingerbread, crumbled
1 (16 ounce) can pumpkin
1 teaspoon ground cinnamon
$1/4$ teaspoon each of ground nutmeg, ginger, and allspice
2 $1/2$ cups milk
4 ($3/4$ ounce) packages instant butterscotch pudding mix
2 cups whipping cream

Set aside $1/4$ cup cake crumbs for topping. Divide remaining crumbs into four portions; sprinkle one portion into bottom of a trifle bowl or 3 quart serving bowl. In large mixing bowl, combine pumpkin, spices, milk and pudding mixes. Mix until smooth. Spoon half into the serving bowl. Sprinkle with a second portion of crumbs. Whip cream until stiff; spoon half into bowl. Sprinkle with a third portion of crumbs. Top with remaining pumpkin mixture, then last portion of crumbs and remaining whipped cream. Sprinkle reserved crumbs on top, around edge of bowl. Cover and chill at least 2 hours before serving.

"Made by our school librarian. Everyone raved about it!"

Linda Hsieh   **Rowland High School, Rowland Heights, CA**

Children's Thanksgiving Cookie Craft

Serves: many   *Dessert*

gingerbread cookies
large gum drops
orange slice candies
candy corn
red gummy worms
whole cloves
small gum drops
Royal Decorator's Icing

Set one gingerbread cookie on a plate, top side up, to make the base. Using frosting like cement, put a dab on bottom of a large gum drop and set on cookie base, near front edge. Frost the bottom of an orange slice and set on base behind gum drop. Cement another cookie, topside facing you, standing up behind orange slice so it creates a fantail. Dab frosting on the back of candy corn and press onto tail so they resemble feathers. Press two candy corns on either side of gumdrop so they resemble wings. Press cloves into either side of the small gum drop to resemble eyes. Using scissors, cut gummy worm into a strip to resemble the comb that will dangle over the top of the head. Secure with frosting. Dab frosting on bottom of head and press it to the top of the large gum drop. Voila! A Turkey!

"A family holiday tradition when my children were young.
My Parenting Class make them every year."

Sandy Massey   **Mountain View High School, El Monte, CA**

Hanukkah

Noodle Kugel

Serves: 15   *Vegetable/Side Dish*

1 (12 ounce) bag wide noodles
1 stick butter, divided
1 cup apricot pineapple preserves
3 ounces cream cheese
$3/4$ cup milk
3 eggs
$1/2$ cup sugar
splash lemon juice (optional)
3 cups corn flakes
cinnamon

Preheat oven to 350 degrees. Prepare noodles as package directs; drain and set aside. Melt butter in a 9" x 13" baking pan; pour off half of butter and set aside. Place cooked noodles on top of butter in pan. Using a mixer or blender, mix together preserves, cream cheese, milk, eggs, sugar and splash lemon juice, if using. Pour over noodles. Crush corn flakes and sprinkle over noodles. Pour remaining melted butter over corn flakes and sprinkle with cinnamon. Bake 50 to 60 minutes or until knife inserted in center comes out clean.

"A must at Hanukkah or anytime. Kugels may be sweet or savory."
Shelly Wellins   **Bolsa Grande High School, Garden Grove, CA**

Blintze Soufflé

Serves: 3 - 4   *Meatless Entreé*

12 frozen blintzes (cheese or fruit)
$1/4$ pound margarine, melted
cinnamon
4 eggs
$1/2$ cup sugar
1 teaspoon vanilla
1 $1/2$ cups sour cream

Preheat oven to 350 degrees. Dip blintzes in melted margarine to coat all sides. Arrange in 9" x 13" pan, about 1" apart. Sprinkle with cinnamon. In blender, combine eggs, sugar, vanilla and sour cream. Pour over blintzes. Bake 40 minutes or until mixture is set.

"The best blintzes you've ever tasted with very little work on your part!"
Susan Eckert   **Las Vegas High School, Las Vegas, NV**

Apricot Sour Cream Kugel

Serves: 10   *Dessert*

1 (12 ounce) package noodles
4 eggs
3 ounces cream cheese, softened
4 ounces butter, melted
$1/4$ cup sugar
1 cup apricot nectar
1 teaspoon vanilla
8 ounces sour cream
Topping:
1 teaspoon cinnamon
$1/4$ cup sugar
2 cups corn flakes, crushed
4 ounces butter

Preheat oven to 350 degrees. Cook and drain noodles according to package directions. Place cooked noodles in a 9" x 13" baking dish. Combine cream cheese with butter, sugar, nectar, vanilla and sour cream. Pour over noodles. Mix cinnamon, sugar and corn flakes and sprinkle on top. Dot with remaining butter. Bake 1 hour.

"Thanks to Marci for her recipe."

Nancy Earnest   **Victor Valley High School, Victorville, CA**

Hanukkah Dreidel Brownies

Makes: 1 large dreidel or 3 dozen brownies   *Dessert*

1 cup butter or margarine
2 cups sugar
2 teaspoons vanilla

> **Photo opposite**
> **page 17**

4 eggs
$3/4$ cup Hershey's Cocoa or Hershey's Dutch Processed Cocoa
1 cup all-purpose flour
$1/2$ teaspoon baking powder
$1/4$ teaspoon slat
1 (10 ounce) package Hershey's Premier White Chips, divided
1 tablespoon shortening (not butter, margarine, spread or oil)
1 (4.25 ounce) tube royal blue decorating icing, optional

Heat oven to 350 degrees. Line a 9" x 13" x 2" baking pan completely with foil, leaving extra on sides for handles. Place butter in large microwave-safe bowl. Microwave on HIGH 2 to 2 $1/2$ minutes or until melted. Stir in sugar and vanilla. Add eggs, one at a time, beating well with spoon after each addition. Add cocoa; beat well until blended. Add flour, baking powder and salt; beat well. Pour batter into prepared pan and bake 30 to 35 minute or just until brownies begin to pull away from sides of pan. Cool completely in pan on wire rack. Invert brownie onto serving tray; peel off foil. Shape into dreidel: About 3" from bottom of each long side, cut triangular pieces to bottom center, forming point of dreidel. Cut about 1" from top edge; cut in half and attach 1 piece as handle. Place 1 cup white chips and shortening in small microwave safe bowl. Microwave on HIGH 1 minute, stirring until melted and smooth. Spread on dreidel, about 1" from top and two sides, forming 7 inch squares. Decorate with remaining white chips and decorating icing, if desired. Cut into bars.

Hershey Foods **Hershey, PA**

Christmas

Christmas Cheese Tree

Serves: 12   *Appetizers & Beverages*

   8 ounces cream cheese
   8 ounces cheddar cheese, shredded
   1 tablespoon red pepper, chopped
   1 tablespoon onion, chopped
   2 teaspoons Worcestershire sauce
   1 teaspoon lemon juice
   dash red pepper
   Garnish: thinly sliced zucchini, fresh flat-leaf parsley,
      pomegranate seeds

Mix cream cheese and cheddar cheese with electric mixer until blended. Blend in remaining ingredients; refrigerate overnight. Drop 6 ($1/3$ cup) dollops of mixture into triangle shape on serving platter. Dollop remaining mixture at base of triangle. Smooth to form a Christmas tree. Garnish with twisted, thin, lengthwise slices of zucchini, parsley and pomegranate seeds. Serve with bread or crackers.

Rebecca Zavala   **Selma High School, Selma, CA**

Christmas Crab Appetizer

Serves: 12   *Appetizers & Beverages*

   Bottom layer:
   8 ounces cream cheese
   1 tablespoon lemon juice
   1 tablespoon Worcestershire sauce
   2 tablespoons onion, grated
   $1/8$ teaspoon garlic powder
   Middle layer:
   3 ounces horseradish
   $1/2$ cup catsup
   1 tablespoon hot sauce
   Top layer:
   $1/2$ pound crab meat, flaked or shredded
   chopped parsley
   Assorted crackers, for serving

Christmas

**Jolly Old
St. Nick Cake**

Page 53

Christmas
Pork Tenderloin with Cherry-Cranberry Glaze
Page 45

Blend ingredients for bottom layer and spread on 12" platter. Mix middle layer ingredients together and pour over bottom layer. Spread crab on top and sprinkle with chopped parsley. Serve with assorted crackers.

"Red and green Christmas colors and tasty too!"

Betty Plooy   **Vanden High School, Fairfield, CA**

Christmas Wreath Punch & Ice Ring

Serves: 40 - 50   *Appetizers & Beverages*

   water
   orange wedges
   red and green maraschino cherries
   3 (12 ounce) cans frozen orange juice concentrate
   1 $1/2$ cups corn syrup
   5 quarts ginger ale, chilled
   $1/4$ cup lime juice

Fill a 6 cup ring mold $2/3$ full with water; freeze. Alternate orange wedges, peel side down, with red and green cherries (3 in each row) on top of ice. Add thin layer of water and freeze 30 minutes more or until fruit is firmly in place. Slowly add water to top; freeze. To unmold, run warm water on sides of mold. Combine orange juice concentrate, corn syrup and lime juice; mix thoroughly. Just before serving, add ginger ale and ice ring.

"Students love this punch and are fascinated by the ice ring. You can add more ginger ale than suggested to taste. To make an all occasion punch, just leave out the cherries and add lime or lemon wedges to ice ring."

Jackie Williams   **Prospect High School, Saratoga, CA**

Cranberry Tea

Makes: 1 $1/2$ gallons   *Appetizers & Beverages*

   1 pound fresh cranberries
   5 quarts water, divided
   2 $2/3$ cups sugar
   $1/2$ cup red hot candies
   8 whole cloves
   juice of 3 lemons
   juice of 3 oranges
   1 cup pineapple juice

Cook cranberries in 2 quarts of water for 40 minutes; strain. Boil sugar, red hots and cloves in 1 quart of water until red hots dissolve. Add mixture to cranberries. Add remaining 3 quarts of water, juice from lemons and oranges and pineapple juice to mixture. Heat to boiling, then reduce heat to simmer. Serve hot.

Stefanie Doke   **Serrano Intermediate School, Lake Forest, CA**

Crescent Veggie Trees

Serves: 32   *Appetizers & Beverages*

2 (8 ounce) cans refrigerated crescent rolls
1 (8 ounce) package cream cheese, softened
$1/2$ cup sour cream
1 teaspoon dried dill weed
$1/8$ teaspoon garlic powder
3 cups assorted vegetables, finely chopped
    (such as bell pepper, broccoli, carrot, cucumber, green onion)

Heat oven to 375 degrees. Remove dough from cans in rolled sections (2 sections from each can). Do not unroll. Cut each into 8 slices (16 slices from each can). Place slices, cut side down onto ungreased cookie sheets to form trees. Start by placing 1 slice for top, arrange 2 slices just below, with sides touching. Continue arranging a row of slices, then 4, ending with a row of 5 slices. Use remaining slices for the trunk. Bake 11 to 13 minutes, until golden brown. Cool 1 minute. Place each tree on a platter. In a small bowl, combine cream cheese, sour cream, dill and garlic powder. Blend until smooth. Spread mixture over both trees. Decorate trees with assorted vegetable pieces. Refrigerate until serving time. To serve, just pull apart the slices of the trees!

"Use colorful vegetables. It's a great Christmas appetizer!"

Gale Hooper   **Casa Roble High School, Orangevale, CA**

Make-Ahead Holiday Meat Balls

Makes: 1 pound   *Appetizers & Beverages*

Meatballs:
1 pound ground meat
1 egg
1 tablespoon soy sauce
$1/2$ cup corn flakes crumbs
dash pepper
$1/4$ teaspoon garlic powder
3 tablespoons catsup
1 tablespoon minced onion
3 tablespoons dried parsley
Sauce:
8 ounces jellied cranberry
6 ounce bottle chile sauce
1 tablespoon brown sugar
2 teaspoons lemon juice

Preheat oven to 350 degrees. Mix meatball ingredients together and form into balls, one tablespoon each. Bake in uncovered baking dish 20 to 30 minutes. Meanwhile, prepare sauce: Combine ingredients in saucepan; heat until melted. Add meatballs to sauce; serve in chafing dish with toothpicks.

Karen Barker   **Prospect High School, Saratoga, CA**

Soft Smokey Cheese Ball

Makes: 1 ball   *Appetizers & Beverages*

$3/4$ cup Cheez Whiz
6 ounces cream cheese
1 teaspoon Worcestershire sauce
$1/8$ teaspoon smoke flavor (or more)
1 cup cheddar cheese, shredded
$1/2$ cup fresh parsley, chopped
$1/2$ cup pecans or walnuts, chopped

In a 1 $1/2$ quart glass bowl, microwave Cheez Whiz 1 minute on HIGH. Add cream cheese and cook 1 to 1 $1/2$ minutes more. Add Worcestershire sauce and smoke flavor and mix well. Stir in cheddar cheese and chill 15 to 30 minutes in freezer or 1 hour in refrigerator. Form into large ball. Combine parsley with nuts; roll cheese ball in parsley-nut mixture.

"Makes a nice gift also when packed with a box of crackers."

Penny Niadna   **Golden West High School, Visalia, CA**

Sun Dried Tomato Pesto & Cheese Spread

Serves: 12   *Appetizers & Beverages*

12 slices Provolone cheese
1 (8 ounce) container cream cheese
1 (small) jar pesto
1 (small) jar sun-dried tomato spread

Line a small bowl with plastic wrap. Line plastic wrap with cheese slices. Spread a thin layer of cream cheese over Provolone. Spread some pesto on cream cheese. Layer a slice of Provolone. Press down. Layer with cream cheese, then sun-dried tomatoes. Put a slice of Provolone on tomatoes. Press down. Repeat cream cheese, pesto, Provolone, cream cheese, tomatoes, Provolone, until all ingredients are gone. At the end, press plastic wrap down tightly over all. Refrigerate overnight. To serve, peel top of plastic wrap and invert onto serving plate. Enjoy with French bread or crackers.

"A delicious recipe from my Aunt Pam. I get asked for the recipe every time. It makes a beautiful presentation for any holiday."

Maria Montemagni   **Mt. Whitney High School, Visalia, CA**

Wassail

Serves: 30 ***Appetizers & Beverages***

1 gallon apple juice or cider
1 (46 ounce) can pineapple juice
6 cups orange juice
2 cups lemon juice
2 teaspoons whole cloves
4 sticks whole cinnamon
sugar or honey, as desired

Heat all ingredients together, until hot, adding sugar or honey to desired sweetness. Before serving, remove cloves and cinnamon sticks. Serve warm. Note: Variations on the amounts of juices can be made subject to availability or personal taste. This also looks nice with orange slices floating on top.

"Great on cold winter days! May cure sore throats too! From the medieval Christmas comes the Wassail bowl. Wassail is from two Anglo-Saxon words: Wes, meaning BE THOU, and Hal, meaning WHOLE."

Peg Ellington **Yucca Valley High School, Yucca Valley, CA**

Apple Pecan Tea Ring

Makes: 2 large rings ***Breads/Baked Goods***

Dough:
5 1/2 to 6 1/2 cups flour
1/2 cup sugar
1 1/2 teaspoons salt
2 packages active dry yeast
1/2 cup margarine, softened
1 1/2 cups water, very hot
2 eggs, room temperature
Filling:
2 cups apples, peeled, chopped
3/4 cup sugar
1 teaspoon cinnamon
1/2 cup pecans or walnuts
4 tablespoons margarine
Frosting:
Ready-made Cream Cheese frosting
Candy sprinkles, red and green

Mix 2 cups flour, sugar, salt and yeast. Add softened margarine. Gradually add water and beat 2 minutes at medium speed, scraping bowl occasionally. Add eggs and 1/2 cup flour or enough to make a thick batter. Beat at high speed. Stir enough additional flour to make a soft dough. Knead on lightly floured board until smooth and elastic, 8 to 10 minutes. Cover with plastic wrap, then a towel and let rest 20 minutes. Meanwhile, mix apples, sugar, cinnamon and nuts. Punch down dough and divide in half. Roll half into an 8" x 16" rectangle. Brush with melted or softened margarine. Sprinkle with apple mixture. Roll up from long side. Pinch seams together to seal. Place sealed edge down in circular shape on greased, foil-covered round or oblong baking sheet. Seal ends firmly. Cut 2/3" of the way into ring at 1" intervals; turn each section on its side. Continue all around ring. Brush with margarine and cover loosely with plastic wrap. Refrigerate 2 to 24 hours. Let stand 45 minutes at room temperature, then bake at 350 degrees for 20 to 25 minutes. Frost with cream cheese frosting and sprinkle with candy sprinkles.

"I have been making this for Christmas morning breakfast since I was in high school! It may be slightly underbaked and then frozen. Reheat and frost Christmas morning. It makes two, so I give one to my side of the family Christmas Eve, and they have it the next morning."

Janine Walton · Etiwanda High School, Etiwanda, CA

Clam Chowder Beauregard

Serves: 8 - 10 · *Soups*

6 slices lean bacon, diced
2 (large) onions, diced
3/4 cup butter
7 potatoes, peeled, diced in large pieces
2 tablespoons parsley, minced
1/8 teaspoon pepper
8 ounces water
1 (51 ounce) can chopped clams
1 quart half & half

Brown bacon. Add onion and cook until translucent. Add half the butter, potatoes, parsley and pepper. Add water. Drain juice from clams and blend in potato mixture. Simmer until potatoes are soft. Add clams. Stir until heated. Add half & half and remaining butter and heat slowly until very hot. Do not boil. Serve immediately.

"My husband has been making this on Christmas Eve for 20 years. My grown sons still request Dad's delicious chowder!"

Janis Brokaw · Mountain Shadows Middle School, Rohnert Park, CA

Winter Tarragon Tomato Soup

Serves: 4   *Soups*

    1 1/2 cups onion, chopped
    1/2 cup butter
    1 (large) can Italian plum tomatoes
    1/2 cup dry white wine
    1 tablespoon sugar
    1 teaspoon dried tarragon
    salt
    sour cream

In a large saucepan over medium heat, saute onion in butter until it starts to turn gold. This will take about 15 minutes. The onions should be stirred so they take color evenly. Add tomatoes, juice and all and mash down with a potato masher. Add wine, sugar, and tarragon; stir. Cover, turn down heat and simmer 45 minutes; cool. Puree soup in a blender, or through a sieve, into saucepan. Reheat, tasting for salt, and keep warm without boiling until serving time. Serve soup in warmed soup plates. Add a dollop of sour cream to each.

"We now serve this soup on Christmas Eve with grilled cheese sandwiches from sourdough. Never use a can of tomato soup again!"

Julie Shelburne   **Tulare Union High School, Tulare, CA**

Christmas Crunch Salad

Serves: 6 - 8   *Salad*

    4 cups broccoli florets, fresh
    4 cups cauliflower florets, fresh
    1 (medium) red onion, chopped
    2 cups cherry tomatoes, halved
    Dressing:
    1 cup mayonnaise
    1/2 cup sour cream
    1 to 2 tablespoons sugar
    1 tablespoon cider vinegar
    salt and pepper, to taste

Combine vegetables in large bowl. Whisk dressing ingredients until smooth. Pour dressing over vegetables and toss to coat. Cover and chill at least 2 hours.

"I enjoyed this delicious salad at the home of my friend, Pam Snow, another FACS teacher. We all really do pass around good recipes!"

Gayle Grigg   **Hendrix Junior High School, Chandler, AZ**

Cranberry Jello Salad

Serves: 10   *Salad*

1 (3 ounce) package strawberry jello
1 $1/2$ cups boiling water
1 cup cranberries, chopped
$1/2$ cup sugar
1 apple, peeled, diced
1 cup celery, chopped

Dissolve jello in boiling water; add cranberries and sugar. When cooled, add apples and celery. Refrigerate until set.

"Sugar can be replaced with non-caloric sweetener.
My piano teacher made this for my sister and me when we were children.
It has been a family favorite every Christmas ever since."

Suzi Schneider   Bret Harte High School, Angels Camp, CA

Crunchy Romaine Salad

Serves: 6   *Salad*

1 $1/2$ heads romaine lettuce
1 head broccoli
3 green onions
1 package Top Ramen
1 cup walnuts, chopped
4 tablespoons butter
1 cup oil
1 cup sugar
$1/2$ cup wine vinegar
3 teaspoons soy sauce
salt and pepper, to taste

Chop lettuce, broccoli and green onions. Toast noodles and walnuts in butter; drain well on paper towels; toss with greens. Combine remaining ingredients in a jar with tight fitting lid; shake well to mix. Pour on top of salad and serve.

"My Aunt Tess Camagna has made this salad at Christmas for years!"

Anne Cornell   Pitman High School, Turlock, CA

Fiesta Corn Salad

Serves: 6 - 8   *Salad*

2 (large) cans whole-kernel corn
2 (large) cans fiesta-style corn
4 stalks green onion, chopped
2 (large) tomatoes, chopped
mayonnaise

Drain corn; combine with onion and tomato in large mixing bowl. Add enough mayonnaise to coat all ingredients. Refrigerate up to 1 day ahead of serving.

"Fast, colorful and delicious. I got the recipe from my sister-in-law, Kay. It's also refreshing on a hot day."

Sharon Both   **Azusa High School, Azusa, CA**

Five Cup Fruit Salad

Serves: 8 - 10   *Salad*

    1 cup Mandarin oranges
    1 cup pineapple chunks
    $1/2$ cup Maraschino cherries, cut in half
    1 cup miniature marshmallows
    1 cup sour cream
    $1/2$ cup coconut, shredded (optional)
    $1/2$ cup walnuts, chopped (optional)

Drain fruit thoroughly. Mix all ingredients together; chill 12 to 24 hours before serving.

"A little goes a long way. It's very rich; easy but elegant."

Sue Fullmer   **Mojave High School, N. Las Vegas, NV**

Lemon Lime Jello Salad

Serves: 8 - 10   *Salad*

    1 package lemon lime jello
    2 cups miniature marshmallows
    2 cups pineapple tidbits, drained
    4 bananas, sliced
    2 cups pineapple juice
    2 eggs
    4 tablespoons flour
    1 cup sugar
    1 cup sour cream
    sharp cheddar cheese, grated

Prepare jello according to package directions; stir in marshmallows, pineapple and bananas. Pour into 9" x 13" dish. Let mixture set. In saucepan over low heat, combine pineapple juice with eggs, flour and sugar. Cook, stirring, until mixture becomes thick, being careful that eggs don't cook too much. Add sour cream. Spread onto jelled salad. Top with grated cheddar cheese, for color.

"This is a favorite side dish for our holiday dinners."

Myrna Westmoreland   **Grace Davis High School, Modesto, CA**

Broccoli Bake

Serves: 6   *Vegetable/Side Dish*

2 packages broccoli, frozen, chopped
1 cup sharp cheddar cheeses, grated
1 can cream of mushroom soup
1 cup mayonnaise
1 1/2 teaspoons dried onion
2 eggs, beaten
1/2 cup almonds, blanched
2 cups bread crumbs
2 tablespoons butter, melted

Cook and drain broccoli. Preheat oven to 350 degrees. Combine broccoli
with cheese, soup, mayonnaise, onion, eggs, and almonds. Place in 2 quart
casserole dish. In separate bowl, combine bread crumbs with butter.
Sprinkle evenly over broccoli mixture. Bake, uncovered, 40 minutes.

"I now have to double this recipe! Everyone wants some to take home!"

Vanessa VanAssen   **Fort Bragg High School, Fort Bragg, CA**

Duck Sauce

Makes: 3 1/2 cups   *Vegetable/Side Dish*

2 cups unsweetened applesauce
3 cups brown sugar
1 cup white vinegar
1 cup onion, chopped
2 cloves garlic, finely chopped
2 tablespoons ginger root, finely chopped
1 tablespoon dark soy sauce
1 teaspoon salt
1/4 teaspoon red pepper flakes
1 tablespoon light mustard seed

Use a 2 quart saucepan. Mix all ingredients together and heat to high until
mixture boils rapidly. Turn heat down to medium and cook gently, stirring
frequently. When mixture is consistency of honey, remove from heat and
transfer to sterile jars; seal. When cool, store in refrigerator. Note: I often
quadruple this recipe and make it in a large pot.

"Friends and family look forward to gift jars during the holiday season.
Wonderful over pork or with a bagel and cream cheese."

Jeri Lundy   **Grossmont High School, La Mesa, CA**

Egg Nog French Toast with Fruit Compote

Serves: 8   *Vegetable/Side Dish*

French Toast:
4 cups egg nog
4 (large) eggs
1 teaspoon ground cinnamon
1 teaspoon ground nutmeg
1 (14 ounce) loaf country white bread, halved horizontally,
    each $^1/_2$ cut crosswise into 8 slices (do not use ends)
$^1/_4$ cup unsalted butter, melted
powdered sugar

Fruit Compote:
2 cups apple cider
6 tablespoons light corn syrup
2 tablespoons light brown sugar, packed
8 tablespoons unsalted butter
3 Golden Delicious apples, peeled, cored, cut into $^1/_2$" pieces
2 cups cranberries, fresh or frozen
$^1/_2$ cup + 1 tablespoon sugar

French Toast: Whisk first 4 ingredients in a large bowl. Place bread slices in a single layer in on baking sheet or 2 9" x 13" glass baking dishes. Pour custard over bread, dividing equally. Cover dishes and refrigerate at least 6 hours or overnight. Preheat oven to 450 degrees. Generously butter bottom and sides of 2 large rimmed baking sheets with some of the melted butter. Using a spatula, transfer bread slices to prepared baking sheets. Brush bread with remaining melted butter. Bake 10 minutes. Turn slices over and bake until golden brown and crisp on outside but soft on the inside, about 6 minutes longer. Place slices on serving plate, top with fruit compote. Dust generously with powdered sugar.

Fruit Compote: Whisk apple cider, corn syrup and brown sugar in a heavy large saucepan. Boil over high heat until reduced to 1 cup, about 15 minutes. Add 4 tablespoons butter, whisking until melted. Remove from heat. Melt remaining 4 tablespoons butter in a heavy skillet over medium heat. Add apples and saute 2 minutes. Add cranberries and $^1/_2$ cup sugar. Stir until cranberries begin to pop, about 2 minutes. Stir reduced cider mixture into skillet with cranberries. Boil until reduced to syrup consistency, about 6 minutes. Stir in more sugar, if desired. Note: Can be made 1 day ahead. Cover and refrigerate. Stir over medium heat until heated through. **Do not boil!**

Janet Dukes   Newport Harbor High School, Newport Beach, CA

Holiday Yam Surprise

Serves: 6 — Vegetable/Side Dish

4 cups yams, baked, mashed
1/4 cup brown sugar
1/2 cup granulated sugar
2 eggs, beaten
1/2 teaspoon cinnamon
1/2 teaspoon nutmeg
1/2 teaspoon salt
6 tablespoons butter, melted, cooled
3/4 cup half & half
Topping:
1/2 cup pecans, chopped
3/4 cup corn flakes, crushed
1/2 cup brown sugar
1/4 cup butter, melted

Grease a 1 1/2 to 2 quart dish. Preheat oven to 400 degrees. Stir together yams, sugars, eggs and seasonings in a large mixing bowl with wooden spoon. Stir in melted butter and half & half. Pour into prepared casserole dish and bake 25 minutes. Mix together topping ingredients. Remove from oven and add topping. Return to oven and bake an additional 10 minutes.

DeeAnn Verdi — North Valleys High School, Reno, NV

Rock Salt Prime Rib

Serves: 10 - 12 — Beef Entreé

rock salt
prime rib roast
1/2 cup water

Preheat oven to 500 degrees. Line a roasting pan with foil and cover bottom of pan with rock salt. Place roast in pan and cover completely with rock salt, pressing salt into roast. Sprinkle with water. Bake, uncovered at 500 degrees, 12 minutes per pound. Remove from oven. Hammer off rock salt and serve.

"Great prime rib!"

Sharron Maurice — Blythe Middle School, Blythe, CA

43

Christmas Morning Oven Omelette

Serves: 12   *Pork Entreé*

- 14 eggs
- $3/4$ cup milk
- $3/4$ cup sour cream
- 1 $1/4$ teaspoons salt
- 1 $1/2$ cups mild cheddar cheese, grated
- 1 $1/2$ cups ham, chopped
- $1/2$ can olives, sliced
- $1/2$ carton fresh mushrooms, chopped
- 2 green onions, sliced
- 1 green pepper, sliced
- $1/4$ cup margarine

Preheat oven to 325 degrees. Blend eggs, milk, sour cream and salt.Stir in cheese, ham, olives and chopped vegetables. Melt butter in a 9" x 13" pan. Pour mixture into pan and bake 45 to 50 minutes.

"Great served for Christmas morning brunch."

Rona Culley   **Cottonwood High School, Salt Lake City, UT**

Herb Roasted Pork Tenderloin

Serves: 8   *Pork Entreé*

- $1/4$ cup soy sauce
- $1/4$ cup Worcestershire sauce
- $1/4$ cup vegetable oil
- 1 teaspoon dried thyme
- 1 teaspoon dried marjoram
- 1 teaspoon rubbed sage
- 1 teaspoon garlic powder
- 1 teaspoon onion powder
- 1 teaspoon ground ginger
- 1 teaspoon salt
- 1 teaspoon pepper
- 2 pounds pork tenderloin

Stir together 11 ingredients for marinade. Place in a shallow dish or heavy Ziploc bag. Prick tenderloin with a cooking fork and place in marinade, turning to coat. Cover or seal and place in refrigerator to marinate 2 hours or overnight. Turn several times. Remove tenderloin and discard marinade. Place on rack in roasting pan. Bake 1 hour, 30 minutes or until meat thermometer inserted into thickest portion registers 170 degrees.

"Around Christmas holidays my daughter, Kathleen Scales, prepares this for family and friends."

Marianne Traw   **Ball Junior High School, Anaheim, CA**

Roast Tenderloin with Cherry Cranberry Glaze

Serves: 4 - 6   *Pork Entreé*

1 (16 ounce) can unsweetened tart cherries
cherry flavored juice
4 teaspoons cornstarch
$^1/_4$ cup brown sugar
$^1/_2$ cup dried cranberries
1 teaspoon yellow mustard
2 whole pork tenderloins, a total of about 1 $^1/_2$ to 2 pounds
salt and pepper, to taste

*Photo opposite
page 33*

Drain cherries, reserving juice. Add enough cherry flavored juice to make one cup. In a small bowl, stir cornstarch into 2 tablespoons juice. In small saucepan, combine cornstarch mixture with remaining juice, cherries, brown sugar and cranberries. Cook, stirring until mixture boils and thickens; stir in mustard. Heat oven to 425 degrees. Season pork tenderloin with salt an pepper; roast in shallow pan for 20 to 30 minutes, until internal temperature reads 155 to 160 degrees. Pour glaze evenly over tenderloins during last 10 minutes of roasting time. Serve sliced.

"Serve with a spinach salad, mashed potatoes and warm breadsticks."

National Pork Board   **Des Moines, IA**

Aloha Loaf

Serves: 6   *Dessert*

$^1/_2$ cup margarine
1 cup sugar
2 eggs
1 (large) banana, mashed
2 cups flour
1 teaspoon baking powder
$^1/_2$ teaspoon baking soda
$^1/_2$ teaspoon salt
1 (8 ounce) can crushed pineapple
$^1/_2$ cup coconut, shredded

Preheat oven to 350 degrees. Grease and flour a 9" x 5" x 3" loaf pan; set aside. Cream margarine and sugar until light and fluffy with electric mixer. Add eggs and mix well. Stir in banana. In another bowl, combine flour, baking powder, baking soda and salt. Stir into creamed mixture; mix well. Fold in pineapple, with juice, and coconut. Pour into prepared pan and bake 1 hour, 10 minutes, or until loaf tests done. Let stand 10 minutes. Remove from pan to cool.

*"This recipe came from a Del Monte cookbook we received as a wedding
gift 30 years ago, and it is the best quick bread you'll ever taste!
We make it in class every year at Christmas as mini loaves for gifts."*

Carole Delap   **Golden West High School, Visalia, CA**

Banana Oatmeal Chocolate Cookies

Makes: 3 dozen   *Dessert*

1 $1/2$ cups oats
1 $1/2$ cups flour
1 cup sugar
2 bananas, mashed
$2/3$ cup shortening
1 egg
1 teaspoon salt
1 teaspoon cinnamon
$1/2$ cup baking chocolate chips
1 teaspoon baking soda

Preheat oven 400 degrees. Mix together all ingredients. Drop by rounded teaspoon onto ungreased cookie sheet. Bake 10 minutes.

"A favorite with everyone in Foods classes!"

Joyce Grohmann   **Los Amigos High School, Fountain Valley, CA**

Candied Walnuts

Serves: a crowd   *Dessert*

$1/2$ cup butter
1 cup brown sugar, packed
1 teaspoon cinnamon
4 cups walnut halves

Melt butter in microwave 1 minute on HIGH using a 1 $1/2$ quart casserole dish. Pour brown sugar and cinnamon into butter. Microwave on HIGH 2 minutes; mix. Add walnuts to mixture, stirring well. Microwave 3 to 5 minutes on HIGH. Spread onto waxed paper; cool. Serve hot or cold.

"Scrumptious!"

Marlene Meola   **Norte Vista High School, Riverside, CA**

Cappuccino Fudge

Makes: 36 pieces   *Dessert*

1 (7 ounce) jar marshmallow creme
$1/2$ cup sugar
$2/3$ cup whipping or heavy cream
$1/4$ cup margarine or butter
1 teaspoon instant coffee powder
$1/4$ teaspoon ground cinnamon
$1/4$ teaspoon salt
1 (12 ounce) bag semi-sweet chocolate chips
1 cup hazelnuts or pecans, toasted

46

Line an 8" square baking dish with foil; set aside. In a 2 quart saucepan, combine marshmallow creme, sugar, cream, butter, coffee powder, cinnamon and salt. Bring to a boil over medium heat, stirring constantly. Continue to boil 5 minutes, stirring constantly. Remove from heat. Stir in chocolate chips until smooth. Stir in nuts. Pour into prepared pan. Cover and refrigerate at least 4 hours or overnight. Using foil, lift fudge onto cutting board. Cut into 36 pieces. Note: You can dust the finished fudge with unsweetened baking chocolate.

"I make this recipe for Christmas gifts, and they're always are a big hit!"
Cindy Word   **Joe Walker Middle School, Quartz Hill, CA**

Chocolate Cake Roll

Serves: 10   *Dessert*

Cake:
$1/2$ cup flour
$1/4$ cup sweetened cocoa powder
1 teaspoon baking powder
$1/4$ teaspoon salt
4 eggs, divided
$1/2$ teaspoon vanilla
$1/3$ cup granulated sugar
Filling:
1 quart vanilla ice cream, softened
Glaze:
$1/2$ cup granulated sugar
4 teaspoons cornstarch
dash salt
$1/2$ cup water
1 (1 ounce) square unsweetened chocolate
2 tablespoons butter or margarine
$1/2$ teaspoon vanilla

Preheat oven to 375 degrees. Grease and lightly flour a 1" x 10" x 15" jelly roll pan. Line with waxed paper that has been lightly oiled. Stir together flour, cocoa, baking powder and $1/4$ teaspoon salt. In separate bowl, beat egg yolks with $1/2$ teaspoon vanilla at high speed 5 minutes, or until thick and lemon colored. Gradually add $1/3$ cup sugar, beating until sugar dissolves. In a large mixer bowl, beat egg whites at medium speed until soft peaks form. Fold yolk mixture into whites. Fold flour mixture into egg mixture. Spread batter evenly into prepared pan. Bake 12 to 15 minutes or until toothpick inserted in center comes out clean. While cake is baking, prepare a towel by sprinkling with powdered sugar. Turn baked cake out onto towel. Remove paper. Sprinkle lightly with powdered sugar. Roll up cake, starting at short end. Let cake cool completely. Soften ice cream. Unroll cake. Spread ice cream on cake; reroll and freeze. Prepare glaze: Combine $1/2$ cup sugar, cornstarch and dash salt. Stir in water and chocolate. Cook and stir until thickened and bubbly, and chocolate melts.

Cook 2 minutes more. Remove from heat and stir in butter or margarine and $1/2$ teaspoon vanilla. Frost rolled cake. Freeze until firm.

"Very easy to do, elegant and very good!"

Pat Peck   **Folsom High School, Folsom, CA**

Chocolate Covered Maple Walnut Creams

Makes: 100 pieces   *Dessert*

    1 stick butter, softened
    2 boxes powdered sugar
    $1/4$ teaspoon maple flavoring
    1 can sweetened condensed milk
    1 cup walnuts, finely chopped
    $1/2$ block paraffin wax
    1 (12 ounce) package chocolate chips

Thoroughly mix together butter, powdered sugar, maple flavoring, sweetened condensed milk and walnuts; chill 2 hours. Form into 1" balls and place on cookie sheets. Chill 2 hours more. Melt paraffin wax in the top of a double boiler with hot (not boiling) water in the bottom pan. Add chocolate chips and stir until melted. Turn off heat. Use a toothpick to remove chilled candy balls from the cookie sheet. Dip into melted chocolate to entirely coat candy. Place on cookie sheet to cool.

Jill Sweet-Gregory   **Santa Paula High School, Santa Paula, CA**

Chocolate Peanut Butter Dreams

Makes: 2 dozen   *Dessert*

    $1/2$ cup butter
    $1/2$ cup peanut butter
    $1/2$ cup sugar
    $1/2$ cup brown sugar
    1 egg
    1 $1/2$ cups flour
    $3/4$ teaspoon baking soda
    $1/2$ teaspoon salt
    $1/2$ teaspoon vanilla
    1 package bite-sized Reese peanut butter cups, unwrapped

Preheat oven to 375 degrees. Cream butter, peanut butter and sugars together. Beat in egg. Mix flour, soda and salt. Blend into creamed mixture. Add vanilla. Shape dough into 1" balls and put in small muffin tins. Bake 8 minutes. Press 1 peanut butter cup into each cookie until only the top of the candy shows. Cool completely. Note: I line my muffin tins with liners to match the occasion.

"Make sure you remove candy from wrappers before baking dough balls. It takes a few minutes to do...longer if you sample along the way! It wouldn't be the holidays without these cookies!"

Barbara Correia   **Foothill High School, Pleasanton, CA**

Chocolate Top Oatmeal Cookies

Makes: 4 dozen   *Dessert*

1 cup + 2 tablespoons butter, divided
$1/2$ cup brown sugar
1 egg
1 cup flour, sifted
1 cup rolled oats
1 (6 ounce) milk chocolate bar
$1/2$ cup nuts, chopped

Preheat oven to 350 degrees. Cream 1 cup butter with sugar; beat in egg. Add flour and rolled oats. Spread in greased 9" x 13" baking pan. Bake 20 minutes. **Do not overbake.** Cool 10 minutes. Melt chocolate bar with remaining 2 tablespoons butter. Spread over cooled cookie, then sprinkle with chopped nuts.

"This is a recipe my mom or sister makes every Christmas. It's different yet easy."

Diane Castro   Temecula Valley High School, Temecula, CA

Crisp Butter Cookies

Makes: 2 dozen   *Dessert*

$1/2$ cup butter, softened
$1/2$ cup margarine, softened
1 cup sugar
1 egg, separated
2 teaspoons vanilla
2 cups flour
$1/2$ cup walnuts, chopped

Preheat oven to 350 degrees. Cream butter, margarine and sugar; add egg yolk and vanilla. Gradually stir in flour. Spread batter onto an ungreased cookie sheet using the palm of your hand. Beat egg white slightly and brush on top of the dough. Sprinkle nuts over top and press into dough. Bake 20 minutes. Remove from oven and cut while hot. Allow to cool. Cookies will crisp as they cool.

"My friend, Blanche Benson, used to make these when we were roommates in college. I couldn't wait until they were out of the oven!"

Pat Hufnagel   Esperanza High School, Anaheim, CA

Date Bars

Makes: 24 - 30   *Dessert*

1 pound pitted dates, cut up
$1/4$ cup sugar
1 $1/2$ cups water
$1/2$ cup margarine
$1/4$ cup shortening
$1/2$ cup brown sugar
1 $3/4$ cup flour
$1/2$ teaspoon baking powder
1 $1/2$ cups oats

Preheat oven to 350 degrees. In saucepan, combine dates with sugar and water. Cook over low heat, stirring until mixture thickens. Set aside to cool. Mix together margarine, shortening, brown sugar, flour, baking powder and oats. Grease a glass 9" x 13" x 2" pan. Press half of the mixture evenly in the bottom of pan and up sides slightly. Spread date filling over crust and top with remaining crumble mixture. Press lightly. Bake 25 to 30 minutes. Cut while warm.

"A special favorite from my mother."

Becky Oppen   **Dana Hills High School, Dana Point, CA**

Easy Cake Mix Cookies

Makes: 2 dozen   *Dessert*

1 box cake mix, any flavor
$1/2$ cup oil
2 tablespoons water
2 eggs
1 $1/4$ cups chocolate chips
(semi-sweet, milk chocolate, white chocolate or any combination)

Preheat oven to 350 degrees. Mix cake mix with oil, water and eggs until well blended. Stir in chocolate chips. Drop by teaspoonfuls onto cookie sheet. Bake 10 minutes. **Do not overbake!** Let cool on cookie sheet. Store in airtight container. Note: For variety, use M&M's in holiday colors, or other chopped candy pieces. Add $1/2$ to 1 cup coconut or nuts if desired.

"This recipe is from my friend, Judy Rose.
It's so quick, so versatile and both kids and adults love the results!

Barbara Schollenberg   **Davis High School, Modesto, CA**

Frozen Pumpkin Squares

Serves: 12 - 16   *Dessert*

  1 (1 pound) can pumpkin
  1 cup sugar
  1 teaspoon salt
  1 teaspoon ground ginger
  1 teaspoon cinnamon
  $1/2$ teaspoon nutmeg
  1 cup pecans, toasted, chopped
  $1/2$ gallon vanilla ice cream, softened
  1 box gingersnaps

Combine the first 7 ingredients. Fold in ice cream. Line bottom of a 9" x 13' pan with gingersnaps. Layer half of the mixture in the pan. Add another layer of gingersnaps. Top with remaining pumpkin mixture. Freeze overnight. Remove from freezer 15 to 30 minutes before serving.

"This is a great substitute for pumpkin pie."

Toni Purtill   **Basic High School, Henderson, NV**

Gingersnaps

Makes: 4 dozen   *Dessert*

  1 cup brown sugar
  $3/4$ cup oil
  $1/4$ cup light molasses
  2 egg whites
  2 cups flour
  2 teaspoons baking soda
  1 teaspoon ground ginger
  $1/2$ teaspoon ground cloves
  $1/4$ teaspoon salt
  granulated sugar, for rolling cookies

Preheat oven to 375 degrees. Combine first four ingredients and beat well. Stir together next five ingredients. Gradually blend second mixture into the first mixture. Using about 1 tablespoon for each, form into balls. Roll in granulated sugar and place on greased cookie sheet about 2" apart. Bake 10 to 12 minutes.

"This is a good no cholesterol family favorite.
We like our gingersnaps chewy, so I bake them 10 minutes or less."

Judie Huffman   **Mariposa County High School, Mariposa, CA**

Grandma's Fudge

Makes: 12 dozen 1" pieces   *Dessert*

5 cups sugar
1 cup margarine
1 (13 ounce) can evaporated milk
18 ounces chocolate chips
1 $^1/_2$ jars marshmallow creme
1 $^1/_2$ cup pecans, broken

Combine sugar, margarine and evaporated milk; cook until it boils, then cook 12 minutes until candy forms medium ball stage. Remove from heat. Stir in chocolate chips, marshmallow creme and nuts. Pour into a 11" x 15" jelly roll pan and allow to cool. Cut into 1" squares. Note: To make clean up easier, I butter the pot and jelly roll pan with margarine before I start to melt it in the pan.

"This is my mother's fudge recipe. It's so good you can't just eat one piece. She always sends everyone in the family a box for Christmas, even if you live around the world, as my brother does in Japan!"

Charlotte Runyan   **Saddleback High School, Santa Ana, CA**

Grandma's Fudge

Makes: 2 dozen 1" squares   *Dessert*

2 squares unsweetened baking chocolate
2 cups sugar
$^2/_3$ cup milk
dash salt
2 teaspoons butter
1 teaspoon vanilla

Melt chocolate in the microwave for 20 seconds, then stir. Continue heating in 20 second intervals and stirring until chocolate is smooth. Pour sugar into large saucepan and add melted chocolate, milk and dash of salt. On medium heat, stir mixture gently until sugar dissolves. Attach a candy thermometer to the inside of the saucepan. Turn heat to low and DO NOT STIR. Cook mixture to between 232 and 237 degrees. Using a clean spoon, stir once and pour some of the fudge mixture into a cup of cold water. Do the ball test. Continue cooking if not done. Use a clean spoon for every test. Take off heat and add the butter and vanilla to the top. DO NOT STIR. Let cool. When you can touch the side of the pan comfortably, beat the fudge with a large spoon until it begins to lose its gloss. Pour into a buttered pie plate and cut into squares.

"This is a very special treat used for our Christmas baskets that we give to friends."

Robin Butterfield   **Rio Vista Intermediate School, Fresno, CA**

Heavenly Hot Fudge Sauce

Serves: 6 - 8   *Dessert*

$1/2$ cup butter or margarine
2 ounces unsweetened chocolate OR 4 tablespoons cocoa
    + 1 tablespoon butter
$1/2$ teaspoon salt
3 cups sugar
1 $1/3$ cups evaporated milk

Melt butter or margarine and chocolate. Stir in salt. Add sugar, a little at a time until completely dissolved. Slowly stir in milk. Cook over low heat for a few minutes until sauce thickens. Serve warm.

"Wonderful hot fudge recipe. My family likes it with any kind of ice cream. Great on brownies with vanilla ice cream. For Christmas, it's really good with crushed peppermint candy canes on top."

Camille Hicks   Riverton High School, Riverton, UT

Homemade Peppermint Patties

Makes: 2 - 3 dozen   *Dessert*

2 pounds powdered sugar
1 can sweetened condensed milk
2 $1/2$ tablespoons peppermint extract
2 (24 ounce) packages almond bark chocolate squares
    (available at Wal-Mart)

In large bowl, mix powdered sugar with condensed milk, using a wooden spoon. You may use your hands also. Add peppermint extract, mix well. With a spoon and your hands, make small balls with sugar mixture and place on waxed paper. Flatten with hand or bottom of glass. Let these dry 20 minutes, then turn over to dry again. In microwave melt chocolate squares according to package directions. Dip patties on fork into melted chocolate in bowl, shake a little, then put back on waxed paper to dry.

"Great recipe from a family friend, Karin Olson."

Ruth Schletewitz   Rafer Johnson Junior High School, Kingsburg, CA

Jolly Old St. Nick Cake

Serves: 12   *Dessert*

1 package cake mix with pudding, any flavor
1 can vanilla frosting
1 drop red food color
miniature marshmallows
$1/4$ teaspoon red food color
gum drops
string licorice

> *Photo opposite*
> *page 32*

Heat oven to 350 degrees. Grease and flour a 9" x 13" pan as directed on package. Prepare and bake cake as directed on package. Cool 30 minutes or until completely cooled. Stir 1 drop food color into frosting. Reserve 1/4 cup of the frosting. Frost top of cake with remaining frosting. To make Santa's face and hat, arrange 7 marshmallows in upper left corner of cake to form tassel of hat. Trace a pattern for hat on waxed paper; cut out. Position on cake below tassel. Using toothpick, outline pattern on frosted cake. Remove pattern. Stir 1/4 teaspoon food color into reserved frosting; frost hat. Arrange marshmallows to form brim of hat, beard around face and mustache. (Marshmallow beard will extend to bottom of cake.) Decorate face as desired with gumdrops and string licorice.

Pillsbury Company   **Minneapolis, MN**

Mamie Eisenhower's Fudge

Makes: 5 pounds   *Dessert*

    4 1/2 cups sugar
    2 tablespoons butter
    dash salt
    1 (13 ounce) can evaporated milk
    1 (12 ounce) package semi-sweet chocolate chips
    3 (4 ounce) packages sweet cooking chocolate, broken
    2 cups marshmallow creme
    2 cups walnut or pecans, chopped

Combine sugar, butter, salt and milk in large saucepan. Bring to a boil over medium heat, stirring constantly. Boil 6 minutes, stirring occasionally. In a large mixing bowl, combine chocolates, marshmallow creme and nuts. Pour syrup over chocolate and beat until chocolate is melted. Turn into well greased 9" x 13" pan. Cool several hours or until firm. Cut into squares and store in airtight container.

Pam Ford   **Temecula Valley High School, Temecula, CA**

Minted Nuts

Makes: 3 cups   *Dessert*

1 cup sugar
$1/2$ cup water
2 tablespoon Karo syrup
$1/8$ teaspoon salt
$1/2$ teaspoon peppermint extract
6 (large) marshmallows
3 cups walnut halves

Combine sugar, water, Karo syrup and salt in a heavy saucepan. Cook over high heat until mixture reaches 230 degrees on a candy thermometer. Remove from heat and stir in peppermint extract and marshmallows, until melted. Stir in nuts until coated. Pour out onto waxed paper and separate into pieces when cool enough to handle.

"My grandmother used to make this family favorite at Christmas time."
Kris Haas   **West Jordan High School, West Jordan, UT**

Mom's Fresh Apple Cake

Serves: 9 - 12   *Dessert*

2 $1/2$ cups flour
1 teaspoon baking soda
1 teaspoon salt
2 teaspoons cinnamon
1 cup oil
2 cups sugar
3 cups apple, cored, chopped
2 eggs
1 cup walnuts, chopped
1 teaspoon vanilla
raisins (optional)

Preheat oven to 350 degrees. In large bowl, sift together flour, baking soda, salt and cinnamon. In another large bowl, beat together oil, sugar, apple, eggs, walnuts, vanilla and raisins. Combine with sifted dry ingredients and mix well. Pour into a greased and floured 9" x 13" glass baking dish. Bake 45 minutes or until a toothpick inserted in center comes out clean. Store uncovered (it will become soggy if covered tightly).

"Our family begs for this every Christmas - very quick and easy.
You don't even have to peel the apples!"
Peggy Herndon   **Central Valley High School, Shasta Lake, CA**

Old Fashioned Almond Roca

Serves: 6   *Dessert*

$^1/_2$ cup almonds, slivered
1 cup butter
1 $^1/_4$ cups sugar
2 tablespoons corn syrup
2 tablespoon water
(12 ounce) package milk chocolate chips

Prepare the pan: Grease a jelly roll pan and sprinkle almonds evenly over bottom. In heavy gauge saucepan, combine butter, sugar, corn syrup and water. Cook over medium heat, stirring constantly, until mixture boils. Broil to brittle stage (300 degrees). Remove from heat. This can take up to 30 minutes. Do not rush this process. If you cook at a high temperature, your candy will burn. Pour the cooked mixture onto prepared pan. Sprinkle chocolate chips evenly over the hot candy. Let stand about 5 minutes. Chocolate chips will become shiny and soft. Spread evenly over the hot candy with the back of a large spoon. Cool in refrigerator 20 minutes or on counter for 1 hour. Break into bite-sized pieces. Eat and enjoy!

"This is a favorite recipe of my students.
Each year they come in asking if they get to make Almond Roca."

Pat Freshour   **Foothill High School, Palo Cedro, CA**

Peanut Butter Cup Cookies

Makes: 3 dozen   *Dessert*

1 $^3/_4$ cups flour
$^1/_2$ cup granulated sugar
$^1/_2$ cup brown sugar, packed
1 teaspoon baking soda
$^1/_2$ teaspoon salt
$^1/_2$ cup shortening
$^1/_2$ cup peanut butter
2 tablespoons milk
1 teaspoon vanilla
1 egg
granulated sugar, for dipping
36 (snack size) peanut butter cup candies

Preheat oven to 375 degrees. Combine flour, $^1/_2$ cup sugar, brown sugar, baking soda, salt, shortening, peanut butter, milk, vanilla and egg in a large bowl until stiff dough forms. Shape into 1" balls; roll each ball in granulated sugar. Place the balls 2" apart on ungreased cookie sheets. Bake 10 to 12 minutes or until golden brown. Remove cookie sheets from oven and immediately top each cookie with a peanut butter cup; sink the candy to the bottom of the cookie. Remove cookies to wire racks to cool.

"I get requests for these cookies again and again. They are the best!"

Adriana Molinaro   **Granite Hills High School, El Cajon, CA**

Peppermint Candy

Makes: 1 pound   ***Dessert***

3 ounces or 15 to 20 small red & white peppermint candy canes
1 (12 ounce) bag white chocolate chips
3 ounces semi-sweet chocolate, melted, optional

Put candy into a food processor and process until it has minced down to a powder with small crumbs of candy, nothing over split pea size. You may also put candy canes in a heavy plastic Ziploc bag and use a hammer to crush. Melt white chocolate chips in microwave or in top of double boiler, stirring often until smooth. Stir crushed candy into melted chocolate and spread out thinly on foil. Place in refrigerator until hardened. If desired, decorate the top with a thin drizzling of dark chocolate. Break into pieces and put into a pretty box for gift giving.

"This delicious candy is also one of the easiest recipes around."

Sue Campbell   Marsh Junior High School, Chico, CA

Snowballs

Makes: 4 - 5 dozen   ***Dessert***

1 cup butter, softened
$2/3$ cup powdered sugar
1 $1/2$ teaspoons vanilla
2 $1/4$ cups flour
$1/4$ teaspoon salt
1 cup walnuts, finely chopped
2 cups powdered sugar, for dusting after baking

Preheat oven to 400 degrees. Cream butter and powdered sugar in large mixing bowl. Add vanilla and blend well. Stir in flour, salt and walnuts. Roll dough into 1" balls. Place 1" apart on ungreased cookie sheet. Bake 12 to 14 minutes, or until lightly browned around edges. Cool 2 to 4 minutes, then dust with about 1 cup powdered sugar. Cool completely, then dust again with powdered sugar.

"These melt-in-your-mouth cookies are a holiday favorite in my family!"

Diana Lee   David A. Brown Middle School, Wildomar, CA

Spritz Cookies

Makes: about 3 dozen   ***Dessert***

$1/2$ cup butter
$1/2$ cup margarine
$2/3$ cup sugar
3 egg yolks
2 $1/2$ cups flour
$1/8$ teaspoon salt
1 teaspoon vanilla

Preheat oven to 375 degrees. With an electric mixer at medium speed, cream butter and margarine.Gradually add sugar and mix until smooth and fluffy. Add egg yolks, flour, salt and vanilla, mixing until smooth and well combined. Fill cookie press with dough. Press out desired shapes. Bake on ungreased cookie sheet for 10 to 12 minutes. Note: Cookies can be made into many shapes using a cookie press: Example, food color dyed green Christmas trees,

"The best spritz cookie recipe EVER - my favorite Christmas cookie. My family likes to make green trees with sprinkles that look like colored Christmas lights."

Trisha Ludeman   **Brookhurst Junior High School, Anaheim, CA**

Tender Drop Cookies

Makes: A bunch   *Dessert*

1 cup butter
1 $1/2$ cups sugar
2 (large) eggs
1 cup sour cream
1 teaspoon vanilla
$1/2$ teaspoon almond extract
3 $1/4$ cups flour
1 teaspoon salt
$1/4$ teaspoon baking powder
$1/2$ teaspoon baking soda
Frosting:
2 $1/2$ cups powdered sugar
1 teaspoon almond extract
$1/4$ cup margarine, softened
2 tablespoons half & half or whole milk

Preheat oven to 350 degrees. Cream together butter, sugar and eggs. Stir in sour cream, vanilla and almond extract. In another bowl, sift together flour, salt, baking powder and soda and stir into creamed mixture. Drop dough by rounded teaspoons onto ungreased cookie sheet. Bake 10 minutes. Tops should bounce slightly when touched. Do not let bottoms brown. Remove from oven and carefully place on cooling rack. Allow cookies to cool completely before frosting. Meanwhile, prepare frosting: Mix powdered sugar, almond extract, margarine and half & half or milk together with hand mixer until light and fluffy. Spread on cooled cookies. Store in sealed container. Flavors meld if allowed to store in a container a day or two before serving.

"Tender drops are a holiday tradition."

Kathy Fullenwider   **Reed High School, Sparks, NV**

Whole Wheat Gingerbread Cookies

Makes: 3 dozen   *Dessert*

1 $1/2$ cups sugar
1 cup margarine
$1/3$ cup molasses
1 egg
2 $1/4$ cups flour
1 cup whole wheat flour
2 teaspoons baking soda
2 teaspoons ground ginger
2 teaspoons cinnamon
$1/2$ teaspoon salt
$1/2$ cup red hot candies

Beat sugar and margarine until light and fluffy. Add molasses and egg; blend well. Stir in flours, baking soda, ginger, cinnamon and salt. Refrigerate until firm. Heat oven to 350 degrees. Roll out dough $1/4$" thick. Cut cookies out with cookie cutters. Place on ungreased cookie sheet and decorate with red hot candies. Bake 6 to 9 minutes. Cool 1 minute on pan, then remove from pan.

"These are the very best gingerbread cookies I've ever tasted!"

Debbie Harvey   **Amador Valley High School, Pleasanton, CA**

Whoopie Pies with Filling

Makes: 13 pies   *Dessert*

Whoopie Pies:
1 $1/2$ cups sugar
$1/4$ cup shortening
1 egg
$1/2$ cup cocoa
1 teaspoon vanilla
2 cups sifted flour
$1/2$ teaspoon cream of tartar
$1/2$ teaspoon baking soda
1 teaspoon salt
$3/4$ cup buttermilk
Filling:
2 $1/2$ tablespoons flour
$1/2$ cup milk
$1/2$ cup shortening
$1/2$ cup sugar
$1/8$ teaspoon salt
1 teaspoon vanilla

Whoopie Pies: Preheat oven to 375 degrees. Cream together sugar and shortening until fluffy. Beat in egg and cocoa. Add vanilla. Sift together flour, cream of tartar, baking soda and salt. Add dry ingredients to creamed ingredients alternately with buttermilk; mix well. Drop by teaspoonfuls onto greased cookie sheet. Bake 10 to 12 minutes. Cool. Spread flat sides of cooled cookie with Fluffy Refrigerator Filling and put together in pairs. *Filling:* Place flour in small saucepan; add a little milk to flour and stir to make smooth paste. Add remaining milk. Cook and stir until mixture thickens; cool. In mixing bowl, cream together sugar, shortening, salt and vanilla until light and fluffy. Slowly add cooled paste mixture, beating constantly until light and fluffy.

"These soft cookie sandwiches can be enjoyed any time,
but a favorite at our family holiday parties!"

Beth Leighton   **Helix High School, La Mesa, CA**

Cinnamon Applesauce Ornaments

Makes: 12   *Craft*

1 cup cinnamon
1 tablespoon cloves, ground
1 tablespoon nutmeg
3/4 cup applesauce
2 tablespoons craft glue

Blend together cinnamon, cloves and nutmeg; stir in applesauce and glue. Knead dough until smooth, about 2 minutes. Divide dough into 4 portions and roll out each portion to 1/4" thickness. Cut with cookie cutters. Using a drinking straw, punch out a hold in dough for hanging. Place ornaments on racks or brown paper bags to dry for several days. Turn ornaments daily so they will dry evenly.

Briana Frigo   **El Modena High School, Orange, CA**

Kwanzaa

Kwanzaa Chocolate Cake

Serves: 8 - 12   *Dessert*

Cake:
$^2/_3$ cup butter or margarine, softened
1 $^1/_2$ cups sugar
1 teaspoon vanilla
2 eggs
2 cups all-purpose flour
$^3/_4$ cup cocoa powder
1 $^1/_2$ teaspoons baking soda
1 teaspoon salt
1 (16 ounce) container sour cream
$^3/_4$ cup banana, mashed
1 cup sweetened coconut flakes
$^1/_2$ to 1 teaspoon freshly grated orange peel (optional)
Frosting:
$^1/_2$ cup butter
8 ounces cream cheese
2 cups powdered sugar
$^1/_2$ cup walnuts or pecans, chopped
Garnish: sliced banana, kiwi fruit and tangerine slices

Preheat oven to 350 degrees. Grease and flour 12 cup fluted pan. In large
mixing bowl, beat butter, sugar and vanilla until creamy. Beat in eggs. In
another bowl, stir together flour, cocoa, baking soda and salt; add
alternately with sour cream to creamed mixture, beating until well blended.
Stir in mashed banana, coconut and orange peel, if using. Pour batter into
prepared pan. Bake 55 to 60 minutes or until wooden pick inserted in
center comes out clean. Cool 10 minutes; remove from pan to wire rack.
Cool completely. Prepare frosting: Cream butter and cream cheese
together. Mix in powdered sugar until smooth. Spread over cooled cake.
Sprinkle nuts on top and garnish with fruit on top of cake.

"Celebration cake to share with family and friends."

Alice Claiborne   **Fairfield High School, Fairfield, CA**

New Year's

Chili Love

Serves: 6 - 8   *Appetizers & Beverages*

1 (15 ounce) can Hormel chili with beans
1 (8 ounce) package cream cheese, cut into cubes
tortilla chips or Fritos

Using a microwave safe dish, combine chili with cream cheese cubes. Microwave on HIGH 1 to 2 minutes or until cheese is half melted. Stop and stir; continue to cook until smooth and blended. Serve with tortilla chips or Fritos.

"Brought into my family when my daughter, Staci, married Brian. Brian tells me it was one of his favorite bachelor recipes."

Shirley Blough   **Hillside Middle School, Simi Valley, CA**

Crab Dip

Serves: 10 - 12   *Appetizers & Beverages*

2 (8 ounce) packages cream cheese
1 (4 ounce) can crab
1 (6 ounce) jar Homemade Chili Sauce
crackers

Let cream cheese warm to room temperature. Spread evenly over large tray or platter. Rinse and drain crab. Sprinkle evenly over cream cheese. Spread chili sauce over top and chill. Serve with your favorite crackers.

"A hit at catering events. I always use the brand name chili sauce. Pipe edge of tray with cream cheese, garnish with parsley."

April Rosendahl   **Chino High School, Chino, CA**

Crab & Shrimp Spread

Serves: 14 - 16   *Appetizers & Beverages*

 2 green onions (include green tops)
 1 cup celery
 1 (7 ounce) can crab meat
 1 (7 ounce) can baby shrimp
 1 cup mayonnaise
 1 can cream of mushroom soup
 1 package Knox gelatin
 6 ounces cream cheese, softened
 Your favorite crackers

Finely chop green onions, celery, crab meat and baby shrimp, then mix with mayonnaise. In small saucepan, heat undiluted soup just to boiling. Stir Knox gelatin into soup and keep stirring until a soupy consistency is achieved. Chop cream cheese into chunks and add to soup mixture. Blend cream cheese with soup mixture using wire whisk until smooth. Remove from heat and stir in crab meat mixture; mix well and set aside. Rub 1 quart loaf pan or casserole with mayonnaise. Pour mixture into prepared dish and place in freezer for about 1 hour. Remove when firm and refrigerate until ready to serve. Serve with your favorite crackers.

"This is a family recipe that we serve at special occasions! Really good!"

Nancy Patten   **Placerita Junior High School, Newhall, CA**

Gouda-Stuffed Mushrooms

Serves: 8   *Appetizers & Beverages*

 6 ounces pancetta (Italian bacon) or Canadian bacon, finely diced
 2 tablespoons butter
 1 (small) onion, finely diced
 3 cloves garlic, minced
 1 cup fresh spinach, packed, chopped
 2 cups Gouda cheese, shredded
 $3/4$ cup fresh breadcrumbs
 2 tablespoons fresh basil, chopped
 salt and freshly ground black pepper, to taste
 24 (2") crimini mushroom caps

Preheat oven to 400 degrees. In a medium skillet, saute pancetta or Canadian bacon over medium-high heat until crisp, about 3 minutes. Remove to a mixing bowl; discard fat from skillet. Melt butter in same skillet over medium heat. Add onion and garlic; saute 3 minutes. Stir in spinach; cook until just wilted. Add to pancetta and allow to cool slightly. Stir in cheese, breadcrumbs and basil. Season with salt and pepper. Place mushroom caps on baking sheet. Mound about 2 $1/2$ tablespoons cheese mixture into center of each mushroom cap. Bake 8 minutes. Serve hot.

Kathie Baczynski   **Mt. Carmel High School, Poway, CA**

Swedish Meatballs

Serves: 8 - 12   *Appetizers & Beverages*

1 pound ground beef
$1/2$ pound ground pork or breakfast sausage
2 eggs
$1/2$ cup milk or red wine
$1/3$ cup bread crumbs
1 teaspoon ground sage
1 teaspoon salt
$1/2$ teaspoon pepper
1 teaspoon garlic powder
$1/4$ to $1/3$ cup onion, finely chopped
3 to 4 tablespoons parsley, finely chopped
$1/4$ cup butter

Place all ingredients, except butter, in large bowl and mix thoroughly or use blade on heavy-duty mixer and blend very well. Heat 2 tablespoons butter in large skillet. Using cookie scoop or hands moistened in water, form $3/4$" to 1" diameter balls and fry in pan, turning often or shaking pan to brown all sides and keep round shape. Serve at once.

"Adapted from a favorite meatloaf recipe my mother always made. These meatballs even taste good with spaghetti sauce over pasta! Serve with beet-root dill-weed sour cream salad, potatoes and green beans."

Carla Escola   **Sierra High School, Manteca, CA**

Good Luck Soup

Serves: 10   *Soups*

2 cups mixed dried beans, rinsed
8 cups cold water
1 teaspoon instant chicken bouillon
1 meaty ham bone
1 (medium) onion, chopped
$1/4$ teaspoon black pepper
$1/4$ teaspoon dried marjoram, crushed
$1/2$ teaspoon garlic powder or salt
2 (medium) carrots, sliced
2 stalks celery, chopped
1 cup (or less, to taste) potatoes, chopped
salt and pepper, to taste

Bring first 8 ingredients to a boil; reduce heat, cover and simmer 1 hour, stirring occasionally. Remove ham bone, cool and remove meat; chop coarsely and return to soup. Discard bones. Stir in carrots, celery and potatoes. Cover and simmer 30 minutes more. Season with salt and pepper.

"This is based on tradition of eating black-eyed peas for good luck on New Years. Be sure your bean mixture contains black-eyed peas!"

Pauline Snyder   **Lompoc High School, Lompoc, CA**

Super Bowl

**Super Bowl
Line-up**
Starts on page 68

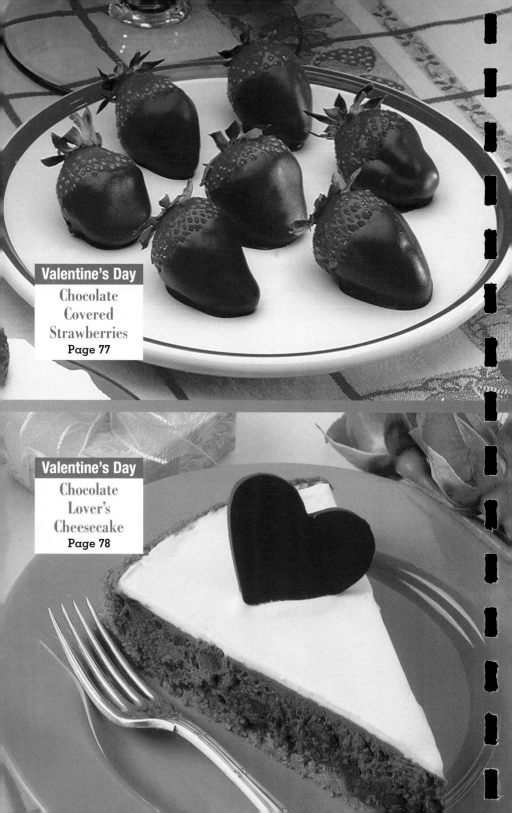

Valentine's Day

Chocolate
Covered
Strawberries
Page 77

Valentine's Day

Chocolate
Lover's
Cheesecake
Page 78

Charlestown Corned Beef Sandwich

Serves: 4 - 6   *Beef Entreé*

1 (2 $1/2$ to 3 pound) corned beef brisket
mustard, to taste
8 to 12 slices dark rye or pumpernickel bread
4 to 6 slices Swiss cheese
$3/4$ to 1 pound deli coleslaw, prepared

Place brisket in large pot, cover with water and add spice packet that comes with the brisket; bring to a boil and simmer 2 $1/2$ to 3 hours. Test for tenderness with fork. Drain and let stand 15 minutes before slicing. Spread mustard on 1 slice of bread. Put 4 to 5 slices meat over mustard. Place 1 slice cheese over meat and top with 2 to 3 spoonfuls of coleslaw. Top with another slice of bread. Cut sandwich in half and serve.

"Named after an area in Boston where my dad grew up, home of the Bunker Hill Monument. Our family's way of celebrating the holiday for two reasons: The meat can be prepared early and served later, and no one likes the smell of corned beef and cabbage in our family."

Janet Policy   **Ramona High School, Riverside, CA**

Navajo Tacos

Serves: 4   *Meatless Entreé*

3 cups flour
1 tablespoon baking powder
1 teaspoon salt
1 $1/2$ cups warm water
1 tablespoon shortening, cut in
3 to 4 cups shortening, melted (for frying)
2 (15 ounce) cans chili beans
2 cups lettuce, finely shredded
1 tomato, chopped
$1/2$ cup onion, chopped
2 cups cheddar cheese, grated
1 cup sour cream
1 cup salsa

Mix first 5 ingredients to form a soft dough and let sit for 10 to 15 minutes. Break off a ball of dough about the size of a golf ball and pat or roll into a flat circle about $1/4$" thick. Fry in 3 to 4 cups melted shortening, until light golden brown. Turn once to brown both sides. Repeat with remaining dough. Heat chili beans. Spoon chili beans over a piece of fried bread and sprinkle with lettuce, tomato and onion. Top with cheese, sour cream and salsa. Enjoy!

"My mom makes this special dish when we come home to visit."

Debbie Jamison   **Sierra Vista High School, Las Vegas, NV**

Whiskey Steak with Roasted Onion Sauce

Serves: 4   *Beef Entreé*

Marinade:
3 tablespoons olive oil
2 tablespoons Dijon mustard
$1/4$ cup bourbon whiskey
$1/3$ cup soy sauce
2 tablespoons red wine vinegar
1 tablespoon A-1 sauce
$1/4$ cup brown sugar
1 tablespoon garlic, minced
2 teaspoons pepper, freshly ground
1 tablespoon red onion, minced
Onion Sauce:
1 sweet onion, cut into 8 wedges
1 teaspoon olive oil
salt and pepper, to taste
$2/3$ cup beef broth
1 teaspoon soy sauce
4 teaspoons cracked black pepper

Mix all marinade ingredients together. Place desired cut of steak in marinade and refrigerate at least 1 hour or overnight, if possible. Grill steaks and serve with Onion Sauce.

Onion Sauce: Preheat oven to 375 degrees. Coat onion wedges with olive oil, sprinkle with salt and pepper. Roast on baking sheet 30 minutes or until soft. In a blender, combine roasted onion with remaining ingredients and blend into a sauce. Pour over barbecued steaks or serve on the side.

Linda Brayton   **Grace Davis High School, Modesto, CA**

Tempura

Serves: 4 - 6   *Seafood Entreé*

$3/4$ cup ice cold water
1 cup Tempura batter mix
vegetable oil, for frying
raw shrimp
fish fillets
raw scallops
green pepper, sliced
sweet potatoes, sliced
carrots, peeled and cut diagonally into $1/4$" thickness
eggplant, sliced
zucchini, unpeeled, cut into $1/4$" slices
green beans or asparagus tips, cut into bite-sized pieces
onion rings

Measure ice cold water into large mixing bowl. Sprinkle batter mix evenly over water. With chopsticks, stir in mix quickly until flour is moist and large lumps disappear. Batter should be very lumpy. Do not stir batter after mixing. Pour vegetable oil for frying at least 2 inches deep into pan. Heat to 375 degrees. Pat seafood and vegetables dry with a paper towel. Dip into batter and gently slide into hot oil. Add only 5 or 6 pieces at a time. Fry until lightly golden brown. Drain on paper towels. Skim off pieces of cooked batter from oil with wire strainer. Serve with dipping sauce or soy sauce. Eat with hot rice.

Reiko Ikkanda   **So. Pasadena Middle School, So. Pasadena, CA**

Super Bowl

Artichoke Appetizer

Serves: 20   *Appetizers & Beverages*

2 jars marinated artichoke hearts
1 (small) onion, chopped
1 clove garlic, minced
4 eggs
$1/4$ cup bread crumbs
$1/4$ teaspoon salt
$1/8$ teaspoon pepper
$1/8$ teaspoon oregano
dash Tabasco
$1/2$ pound cheddar cheese, shredded
2 tablespoons parsley, minced

Preheat oven to 325 degrees. Drain marinade from one jar of artichoke hearts into frying pan. Discard marinade from second jar or set aside for another recipe. Chop artichoke hearts from both jars and set aside. Saute onion and garlic in frying pan until tender. In bowl, beat eggs; add bread crumbs and seasonings. Stir in chopped artichoke hearts and stir in remaining ingredients. Grease 7" x 11" pan. Pour mixture into pan and bake 30 minutes.

Venetta Ramm   **La Habra High School, La Habra, CA**

Cowboy Grub

Serves: 4 - 6   *Appetizers & Beverages*

2 tablespoons red wine vinegar or rice vinegar
1 teaspoon vegetable oil
1 clove garlic, minced
1 can black beans, drained
1 can kernel corn, drained
$1/3$ cup red onion, finely chopped
$1/4$ cup cilantro, chopped
salt and pepper, to taste
grated cheese (optional)
tortilla chips

Mix vinegar, oil, garlic, beans, corn, onion, cilantro and salt and pepper together and heat in medium saucepan 5 minutes. Place in serving bowl, sprinkle with grated cheese and serve with tortilla chips,

"Great to satisfy those hearty appetites on game day!"

Linda Stokes   **Riverton High School, Riverton, UT**

Fiesta Dip

Makes: 2 cups   *Appetizers & Beverages*

    1 (1 ounce) package Lawry's Taco Spices & Seasonings
    2 cups sour cream
    tortilla chips and assorted crisp vegetables

> **Photo on front cover**

In medium bowl, combine Taco Spices & Seasonings with sour cream; mix thoroughly. Cover and refrigerate for about 1 hour. Serve with tortilla chips and crisp vegetables.

Lawry's Foods Inc.   **Monrovia, CA**

First String Mango Salsa

Makes: 5 cups   *Appetizers & Beverages*

    4 ripe mangoes peeled, coarsely chopped
    $1/2$ red onion, peeled, diced
    2 jalapeno peppers, seeded, finely chopped
    4 tablespoons lime juice
    2 cloves garlic, minced
    4 tablespoons fresh cilantro, minced
    2 teaspoons ground black pepper
    salt, to taste

> **Photo opposite page 64**

In a large bowl, stir together all ingredients well; refrigerate at least 1 hour to allow flavors to blend. Note: Use rubber gloves when handling peppers.

National Pork Board   **Des Moines, IA**

Perfect Pecans

Makes: 2 pounds   *Appetizers & Beverages*

    1 stick butter
    2 pounds pecans, shelled
    2 tablespoons Worcestershire sauce
    Lawry's seasoned salt, to taste

Preheat oven to 300 degrees. Melt butter in pan, stir in pecans, Worcestershire sauce and seasoned salt, to taste. Stir to coat. Spread onto baking sheet and bake 10 to 20 minutes, stirring every 5 minutes, until pecans are lightly browned. Drain on brown bag. Store in airtight container.

"I make this recipe for every football party and give it as gifts at Christmas!"

Michelle Miller   **Aliso Viejo Middle School, Aliso Viejo, CA**

Quarterback Quesadillas

Serves: 8   *Appetizers & Beverages*

8 (10") flour tortillas
1 pound cooked pork roast, chopped
1 cup reduced fat Monterey Jack cheese, shredded
1 to 2 jalapeno peppers, seeded, minced
$1/4$ cup onion, minced
4 tablespoons cilantro, minced
$1/4$ teaspoon salt
$1/2$ teaspoon pepper
tomato salsa, homemade or purchased, or fruit salsa

| Photo opposite |
| page 64 |

In large bowl, stir together pork, cheese, peppers, onion, cilantro, salt and pepper. Arrange one-eighth of the filling on each tortilla, covering half of it. Fold tortilla over to make a half-moon. Place on shallow baking pans. Bake in 500 degree oven until tortillas are crisp and golden, about 5 minutes. Transfer to large cutting board and cut into edges to serve with salsa. Note: Use rubber gloves when handling peppers.

National Pork Board   **Des Moines, IA**

Snack Mix with Honey Glaze

Serves: 8 - 10   *Appetizers & Beverages*

4 cups crispy corn squares cereal
1 $1/2$ cups miniature pretzels
1 cup walnut halves (or other nut)
$1/3$ cup butter or margarine
$1/4$ cup honey

Preheat oven to 350 degrees. In a large bowl, combine cereal, pretzels and nuts. Over low heat, melt butter or margarine; stir in honey. Pour over cereal mixture and toss to coat. Spread onto 10" x 15" jelly roll pan. Bake 12 to 15 minutes or until glazed, stirring occasionally. Cool slightly and spread on waxed paper. Cool completely and store in container.

"This is great at Christmas or anytime you want a snack that is easy to make and simple to serve. It would be great for Super Bowl Sunday!"

Kathleen Fresquez   **Mountain View High School, El Monte, CA**

Super Bowl Favorite Wings

Serves: 6 - 8   *Appetizers & Beverages*

    2 to 3 pounds chicken wings, fresh or frozen
    2 to 3 cups brown sugar
    1 (20 ounce) can crushed pineapple
    3/4 tablespoon black pepper
    6 tablespoons soy sauce
    6 tablespoons lemon juice
    2 tablespoons garlic salt or powder

Sprinkle chicken generously with brown sugar. Lay on large cookie sheet, one layer of chicken wings (don't overlap). Distribute the pineapple over the wings. Sprinkle with pepper. Mix soy sauce with lemon juice and drizzle over wings. Sprinkle garlic over all. Bake at 225 degrees for 6 to 8 hours or at 300 degrees for 3 1/2 hours. No turning or basting required.

"An annual favorite on Super Bowl Sunday at our house!"

Paulette Evans   Cyprus High School, Magna, UT

Touchdown Black-Eyed Pea Dip

Makes: 5 cups   *Appetizers & Beverages*

    1 (15 ounce) can black-eyed peas, drained
    1 (15 ounce) can white or yellow hominy, drained
    1/2 cup mild onion, chopped
    1/4 cup fresh cilantro, chopped   *Photo opposite*
    1 cup hot salsa   *page 64*
    2 cloves garlic, minced

In large bowl, stir together all ingredients well; cover and refrigerate to let flavors blend, at least 2 hours or overnight. Serve with lowfat chips as dippers.

National Pork Board   Des Moines, IA

Cheese and Clam Chowder

Serves: 5 - 6   *Soups*

    1 cup water
    1 (8 ounce) can minced clams
    2 cups potatoes, diced
    2 cups carrots, peeled, thinly sliced
    1 teaspoon chicken bouillon
    1 (10.75 ounce) can cream of celery soup
    2 cups milk
    1 1/2 teaspoons seasoning salt
    1 cup Monterey jack cheese, shredded

Pour water and juice from drained clams into saucepan. Add potatoes, carrots and bouillon. Simmer until vegetables are tender. Add cream of celery soup, clams, milk, seasoning salt and cheese. Heat gently; do not boil.

"This may not be a "Super Bowl Soup" unless the
New England Patriots are playing!"

Jan Neufeld   **Fullerton High School, Fullerton, CA**

Nacho Chorizo Casserole

Serves: 6 - 8   *Beef Entreé*

$^1/_2$ pound chorizo
$^1/_2$ pound ground beef
1 can refried beans
1 pound jack cheese, shredded
1 (small) can olives, sliced
1 (8 ounce) can diced green chiles
$^1/_2$ cup sour cream
salsa, to taste
1 avocado, peeled, diced
tortilla chips

Preheat oven to 350 degrees. In a large frying pan, brown chorizo and ground beef; drain fat. In an 8" x 8" pan, layer meats, beans, cheese, olives and chiles. Bake 10 to 15 minutes or until cheese is melted. Top with sour cream, salsa, and avocado. Serve with tortilla chips.

"This is great stuff! We make it in our Foods 2 classes with
homemade tortilla chips, and the students love it!"

Libby Newman   **West Valley High School, Hemet, CA**

Time Out Pork Burros

Serves: 12   *Pork Entreé*

3 cups roast pork, finely shredded or chopped
1 cup onion, chopped
1 clove garlic, minced
1 to 3 tablespoons jalapeño pepper, diced
12 flour tortillas, warmed
3 cups lettuce, shredded
2 cups tomatoes, diced
$^3/_4$ cup cheddar cheese, shredded
salsa, as desired

> ***Photo opposite***
> ***page 64***

In nonstick skillet, sweat onion and garlic over medium heat for 5 minutes, until soft and translucent. Add cooked pork; toss lightly. Heat thoroughly. Stir in jalapeño pepper. In each tortilla, roll up $^1/_4$ cup shredded pork, a portion of the lettuce, tomatoes, 1 tablespoon cheese and top of salsa, if desired. Note: Use rubber gloves when handling peppers.

National Pork Board   **Des Moines, IA**

Winning White Chili

Serves: 6   *Pork Entreé*

$1/2$ pound boneless pork loin (or 2 boneless pork chops)
  cut into $1/2''$ cubes
1 cup onion, chopped
1 teaspoon oil
1 $1/2$ teaspoons ground cumin
$1/4$ teaspoon garlic powder
1 cup wild rice, cooked
1 (16 ounce) can navy beans, drained
1 (16 ounce) can chickpeas, drained
1 (4 ounce) can diced green chiles, drained
1 (16 ounce) can white kernel corn, drained
$1/8$ teaspoon hot pepper sauce
1 (14.5 ounce) can chicken broth
chopped parsley

*Photo opposite
page 64*

In a 4 quart saucepan, saute onion and pork in oil over medium-high heat
until onions are soft and pork lightly browned, about 5 minutes. Stir in
remaining ingredients except parsley. Cover and simmer 20 minutes. Serve
each portion garnished with chopped parsley.

National Pork Board   **Des Moines, IA**

Valentine's Day

Pancakes "From The Heart"

Makes: 6   *Breads/Baked Goods*

1 1/4 cups all-purpose flour
2 teaspoons sugar
1/2 teaspoon salt
1 tablespoon baking powder
1 egg
1 cup milk
2 tablespoons oil

Sift together flour, sugar, salt and baking powder into a mixing bowl. Beat egg, milk and oil together and pour into dry ingredients. Mix with an electric mixer until batter is smooth. Pour batter from a measuring cup to the diameter desired in a lightly oiled pan. Bake until golden brown on the bottom, flip over and bake the other side. Serve at once, or hold in a 150 degree oven with paper towels separating pancakes.

"Pour batter into heart shaped molds for a special
Valentine breakfast. Garnish heart pancakes with strawberries
cut into hearts. Don't forget the butter and syrup!!"

Melissa Webb   **Lakewood High School, Lakewood, CA**

Strawberry French Toast

Serves: 10 - 12   *Breads/Baked Goods*

12 slices bread
2 (8 ounce) packages cream cheese
1 cup strawberries, fresh or frozen
12 eggs
2 cups milk
1/3 cup maple syrup or honey
Syrup:
1 cup sugar
2 tablespoons corn starch
1 cup water
1 cup strawberries
1 tablespoon margarine

74

Cut bread and cream cheese into cubes. Place in a 9" x 13" baking pan. Sprinkle strawberries over top. Beat eggs, then beat in milk and syrup or honey. Pour over top of ingredients in pan. Cover with foil and refrigerate overnight. Remove from refrigerator and bake at 350 degrees for 30 minutes. Remove foil and bake another 30 minutes. While baking, prepare syrup: Mix together sugar and corn starch. Add water and cook, stirring constantly over medium heat until boiling. Add strawberries and cook another 3 minutes. Add margarine and serve.

"Perfect "make ahead" breakfast for everyone you "love" on this special day! You may use blueberries instead of strawberries."

Linda Stokes   **Riverton High School, Riverton, UT**

Spinach Strawberry Salad

Serves: 8   ***Salad***

   1 (large) bag fresh baby spinach leaves
   1 box fresh strawberries, sliced
   1 package slivered almonds
   Dressing:
   $1/2$ cup sugar
   1 $1/2$ teaspoons minced onion
   $1/4$ teaspoon Worcestershire sauce
   $1/4$ cup cider vinegar
   $1/2$ cup oil

Wash and drain spinach leaves. Toss with sliced strawberries and slivered almonds; set aside. Put all dressing ingredients in a blender; blend. Pour over salad. Toss and serve.

"A delicious salad that is a little different. Recipe was given to me by my sister, Stephanie - one great cook!"

Susan Lefler   **Ramona Junior High School, Chino, CA**

Bourbon Chicken

Serves: 6   *Chicken Entreé*

12 pieces chicken
salt, pepper, garlic powder, to taste
2 cups onion, chopped
$1/4$ cup butter
1 bunch green onions, chopped
3 tablespoons parsley, chopped
1 teaspoon garlic powder
$1/2$ teaspoon pepper
2 cups chicken stock, divided
dash Kitchen Bouquet
1 tablespoon sugar
2 ounces bourbon
2 tablespoons cornstarch
3 cups rice, cooked

Preheat oven to 350 degrees. Season chicken pieces with salt, pepper and garlic powder. Bake 45 minutes. Meanwhile saute chopped onion in butter. Add green onion, parsley, garlic powder, pepper, 1 $1/2$ cups chicken stock, Kitchen Bouquet and sugar; simmer 15 minutes. Add bourbon and cook 5 minutes more. Dissolve cornstarch in remaining $1/2$ cup chicken stock and add to thicken sauce. Pour sauce over chicken and return to oven. Bake 30 minutes more. Serve with rice.

"The sauce is terrific. I have substituted pork chops for the chicken with wonderful results. A New Orleans recipe from the Cajun Cooking School."
Laura May   **Lucerne Valley High School, Lucerne Valley, CA**

Black Forest Trifle

Serves: 16   *Dessert*

1 package brownie mix (9" x 13" pan size), prepared
2 packages chocolate mousse mix, prepared
1 can cherry pie filling
1 (8 ounce) carton frozen whipped topping, thawed
4 Skor candy bars, crushed

Prepare and bake brownies; cool on wire rack. Prepare mousse according to package directions. Crumble brownies. Sprinkle half into a 4 quart trifle dish or glass bowl. Top with half of the pie filling, half of the prepared mousse, half of the whipped topping and half of the crushed candy; repeat. Cover and refrigerate 8 hours or overnight.

"This is a great potluck dessert. You won't take any leftovers home!"
Kathy Warren   **McClatchy High School, Sacramento, CA**

Cherry Cheese Pie

Serves: 8   *Dessert*

    1 package Dream Whip
    $1/2$ cup milk
    $1/2$ teaspoon vanilla
    2 (8 ounce) packages cream cheese
    $1/2$ cup sugar
    1 9" unbaked graham cracker crust
    1 can cherry pie filling

Prepare Dream Whip as directed on package using milk and vanilla. Soften cream cheese and beat with sugar until smooth. Blend prepared Dream Whip with cream cheese mixture. Spoon into unbaked crust. Chill 3 hours or longer. Top with cherry pie filling.

Dorothy Jones   **Etiwanda High School, Etiwanda, CA**

Chocolate Covered Strawberries | *Photo opposite page 65* |

Makes: 1 cup   *Dessert*

    2 (12 ounce) packages Hershey's Semisweet chocolate chips
    2 tablespoons shortening (do not use butter, margarine,
        spread or oil)
    fresh strawberries, with stems, rinsed, patted dry

Cover tray with waxed paper. Place chocolate chips and shortening in medium microwave-safe bowl. Heat on HIGH 1 $1/2$ minutes or just until chips are melted and mixture is smooth when stirred; cool slightly. Holding strawberry by stem, dip $2/3$ of each berry into chocolate mixture; shake gently to remove excess. Place on prepared tray. Refrigerate until coating is firm, about 30 minutes. Store, covered, in refrigerator. Note: Coats about 5 dozen small strawberries.

Hershey Foods   **Hershey, PA**

Chocolate Lover's Cheesecake

Serves: 10 - 12   *Dessert*

Graham Crust:
1 $^1/_2$ cups graham cracker crumbs
$^1/_3$ cup sugar
$^1/_3$ cup butter or margarine, melted
Filling:
2 (8 ounce) packages cream cheese
$^3/_4$ cup + 2 tablespoons sugar, divided
$^1/_2$ cup Hershey's Cocoa
2 teaspoons vanilla, divided
2 eggs
1 cup Hershey's Semisweet Chocolate Chips
1 (8 ounce) container sour cream

> **Photo opposite
> page 65**

Preheat oven to 375 degrees. Stir together graham cracker crumbs, $^1/_3$ cup sugar and melted butter or margarine in medium bowl; mix well. Press mixture firmly onto bottom and halfway up sides of 9" springform pan. Beat cream cheese, $^3/_4$ cup sugar, cocoa and 1 teaspoon vanilla in large bowl until light and fluffy. Add eggs, beat until blended. Stir in chocolate chips and pour into prepared crust. Bake 20 minutes. Remove from oven; cool 15 minutes. Increase oven temperature to 425 degrees. Stir together sour cream, remaining 2 tablespoons sugar and remaining 1 teaspoon vanilla in small bowl; stir until smooth. Spread evenly over baked filling. Bake 10 minutes. Remove from oven to wire rack. With knife, loosen cake from side of pan. Cool completely, Remove side of pan. Refrigerate several hours before serving.

Hershey Foods   **Hershey, PA**

Covered with Kisses Chocolate Cherry Torte

Serves: 10 - 12   *Dessert*

$^1/_2$ cup butter or margarine, melted
1 $^1/_4$ cups granulated sugar
1 teaspoon vanilla
2 eggs
$^2/_3$ cup all-purpose flour
$^1/_2$ cup Hershey's Cocoa
$^1/_4$ teaspoon baking powder
$^1/_4$ teaspoon salt
1 (8 ounce) package cream cheese, softened
1 cup powdered sugar
$^1/_2$ cup whipping cream, chilled
1 (10ounce) package Hershey's Mini Kisses Baking Pieces
1 (21 ounce) can cherry pie filling, chilled

> **Photo on cover**

Heat oven to 350 degrees. Grease bottom only of 9" springform pan or line 9" round cake pan with foil; grease bottom of foil. Stir together melted butter, sugar and vanilla in large bowl. Add eggs; using spoon, beat well. Stir together flour, cocoa, baking powder and salt; gradually add to egg mixture, beating with spoon until well blended. Spread batter into prepared pan. Bake 25 to 30 minutes or until cake is set. (Cake is fudgey and will not test done.) Remove from oven; cool completely in pan on wire rack. Beat cream cheese and powdered sugar in medium bowl until well blended. Beat whipping cream until stiff. Gradually fold into cream cheese mixture, blending well. Spread over top of torte; refrigerate several hours or until set. With knife, loosen cake from side of pan and remove, or lift torte out of pan, using foil; remove foil. Just before serving, put baking pieces in 6" wide heart outline in center of cake. Fill heart shape with cherries from pie filling. Put baking pieces all around outside edge. Serve cold, cut into wedges with remaining pie filling. Cover and refrigerator leftovers.

Hershey Foods   **Hershey, PA**

George Washington Easy Cherry Crisp

Serves: 12 - 16   *Dessert*

    2 (21 ounce) cans cherry pie filling
    1 cup flour
    $1/2$ cup butter
    $1/2$ cup sugar
    $1/2$ cup brown sugar
    1 teaspoon cinnamon
    Optional: whipped cream or vanilla ice cream

Preheat oven to 350 degrees. Pour pie filling into a 9" x 13" baking pan. In a small bowl, combine flour and butter. Blend with a pastry blender or a fork. Add sugar, brown sugar and cinnamon. Mix well. Sprinkle over cherries. Bake 30 minutes. If desired, serve with whipped cream or ice cream.

*"Very easy to make and is a good alternative to all the
Valentine candy you'll be eating!"*

Michelle Ferguson   **Hanford West High School, Hanford, CA**

Heart-Shaped Fruit Pizza

Serves: 6   *Dessert*

    1 package Pillsbury sugar cookie dough, at room temperature
    1 package cream cheese, softened
    1 container Cool Whip Lite
    dash vanilla extract (optional)
    1 pint strawberries, washed, sliced
    6 kiwi fruit, thinly sliced
    1 can Mandarin oranges, drained
    Assorted fruit toppings

Roll cookie dough to ¼" to ½" thick. Shape dough into a heart, being careful not to handle too much. Bake according to package directions. Cool 8 to 10 minutes. Mix together cream cheese, Cool Whip and vanilla, (if desired) and spread over cookie crust. Garnish with desired fruit in a decorative fashion. Serve with fruit topping of your choice. Note: If cream cheese mixture is too thick, you may use 1 to 2 tablespoons of milk to soften it.

"This dish is not only good to eat, but a treat for the eyes when you use colorful fruit. "

Jannie Parks   **Ramona High School, Riverside, CA**

Italian Love Cake

Serves: 8   *Dessert*

    1 angel food cake
    ¹/₂ cup Amaretto
    1 pint pistachio ice cream
    1 pint chocolate ice cream
    2 cups heavy cream
    6 ounces semi-sweet chocolate morsels

Cut cake into 3 layers. Sprinkle layers with 6 tablespoons Amaretto. Place one layer on serving platter. Cut ice cream into slices and put pistachio ice cream on bottom layer. Top with second cake layer and a layer of chocolate ice cream. Top with third cake layer. Place in freezer. In bowl, mix heavy cream and remaining Amaretto and beat until very thick. Frost the sides and top with whipped cream mixture and place in freezer. Melt chocolate over very low heat until smooth. Spread chocolate in a ¼" thick layer on foil and chill until it hardens. With a small heart cookie cutter, cut hearts out of chocolate and place on top of cake. Freeze cake until ready to serve.

"Strawberry ice cream can be used in place of chocolate."

Angela Croce   **Mira Mesa High School, San Diego, CA**

Jello Graham Cracker Dessert

Serves: 8   *Dessert*

    2 cups powdered sugar
    ¹/₂ cup margarine
    1 egg
    1 teaspoon vanilla
    ¹/₂ cup walnuts, chopped
    1 (6 ounce) package raspberry jello
    1 cup raspberries
    1 package graham crackers
    whipped cream

Cream together powdered sugar, margarine, egg and vanilla; stir in walnuts. In another bowl, prepare jello according to package directions; stir in raspberries and chill until partially set. Line an 8" x 10" dish or pan with whole graham crackers. Spread creamed mixture on top of crackers and cover with another layer of crackers. Top with jello mixture. Chill. Cut into squares and serve with whipped cream.

"One of my favorite recipes from my Grandmother."

Pat Johnson   **Iron Horse Middle School, San Ramon, CA**

Muffy's Famous Sugar Cookies

Makes: 4 dozen   *Dessert*

    2 cups sugar
    1 cup shortening
    4 eggs
    1 cup milk
    2 teaspoons vanilla
    7 cups flour
    2 teaspoons baking soda
    4 teaspoons cream of tartar

Preheat oven to 350 degrees. Cream sugar and shortening. Add eggs, milk and vanilla. Sift dry ingredients together and add to creamed mixture. Roll out to $1/4$" thickness and cut into desired shapes. Place on cookie sheet and bake 5 to 7 minutes.

"This recipe requires no refrigeration prior to baking!"

Julie Ericksen   **Skyline High School, Salt Lake City, UT**

Rice Krispies Valentine Kiss

Makes: 2 to 4 large kisses   *Dessert*

    $1/2$ stick butter or margarine
    8 ounces miniature marshmallows
    6 cups Rice Krispies cereal

Melt butter or margarine in a large saucepan over low heat. Stir in marshmallows until melted. Turn off heat and add cereal. Stir well until coated. Cool slightly. Spray your hands with nonstick cooking spray and press mixture into large greased funnels and place on a cookie sheet. When cool, unmold and wrap in foil. You may want to add a flag with a message taped to a toothpick.

"These resemble large Hershey's kisses!"

Natalie Henwood   **Riverton High School, Riverton, UT**

Valentine's Cake

Serves: 8 - 12   *Dessert*

   1 cake mix
   Cool Whip
   Candy sprinkles

Prepare and bake cake according to package directions, using (1) 8" or 9" round pan and (1) square pan. Use parchment paper to line pans so cake is easy to remove. When cakes have been removed from pans and cooled, cut round layer in half; leave square layer whole. Place square pan on the diagonal on a large platter or foil wrapped cardboard. Place one half of the round layer on each side, forming a heart. Frost with Cool Whip and sprinkle with candy sprinkles.

Sue Markert   **Swope Middle School, Reno, NV**

Waldorf Astoria Red Cake

Serves: 16   *Dessert*

   $1/2$ cup butter
   1 $1/2$ cups sugar
   2 eggs
   2 ounces red food coloring
   2 teaspoons cocoa
   1 teaspoon salt
   1 cup buttermilk
   2 $1/4$ cups cake flour
   1 teaspoon vanilla
   1 teaspoon baking soda
   1 teaspoon vinegar

Preheat oven to 350 degrees. Prepare 2 9" heart-shaped layer pans by greasing and dusting with flour; set aside. Cream butter and sugar; add eggs and mix well. Make paste of cocoa and red food coloring and add to creamed mixture. Mix in salt and buttermilk, alternating with flour; add vanilla. Mix together vinegar and soda, then fold into batter. Bake in heart pans, 22 to 25 minutes or until center springs back when touched. Cool on wire racks and remove from pans after 10 minutes. Frost with your favorite buttercream frosting.

> *"A lady is said to have asked for this recipe saying*
> *'I'll give a hundred dollars for the recipe'.*
> *The waiter brought back the recipe and a bill for $100!"*

Betty Plooy   **Vanden High School, Fairfield, CA**

St. Patrick's Day

Sea Foam Punch

Serves: 10 - 12   *Appetizers & Beverages*

1 package lemon-lime Kool Aid
1 cup sugar
4 cups milk
27 ounces lemon-lime soda
1 pint vanilla ice cream

In large punch bowl, dissolve Kool Aid and sugar in milk; add soda and stir. Float scoops of vanilla ice cream in punch.

"It's green and foamy! Fun for St. Patrick's Day!"

Dale Sheehan   **Santana High School, Santee, CA**

St. Patrick's Day Scones

Makes: about 1 dozen   *Breads/Baked Goods*

$3/4$ cup flour
1 $1/2$ teaspoons baking powder
$1/4$ teaspoon salt
1 tablespoon sugar
2 tablespoons + 2 teaspoons shortening
$1/4$ cup quick cooking oats
$1/3$ cup milk
$1/2$ teaspoon butter, melted
cinnamon and sugar, to taste

Preheat oven to 450 degrees. Sift flour, baking powder, salt and sugar into mixing bowl. Cut in shortening. Add oats and milk, stir just until blended. Form dough into a ball. Divide dough into two parts. Roll each part about $3/4$" thick with floured rolling pin. Cut out rounds or squares using 2" cookie cutter dipped in flour. Spread each cut-out with melted butter, sprinkle with cinnamon sugar and arrange on cookie sheet about 1" apart. Bake 12 to 15 minutes or until nicely browned.

Joy Sweeney-Aiello   **Exeter High School, Exeter, CA**

Martian Salad

Serves: 6 - 8 *Salad*

1 (6 ounce) box lime jello
1 (15 ounce) can crushed pineapple
1 (16 ounce) carton cottage cheese
1 (8 ounce) carton Cool Whip

Pour dry jello powder into medium bowl. Drain crushed pineapple and stir fruit into jello powder; mix well. Stir in cottage cheese and fold in Cool Whip. Chill 1 hour or more if time permits or serve immediately!

"My children named this salad which made it more fun to eat.... coming from outer space! And they learned to eat cottage cheese!"

Betty Bundy **Hidden Valley Middle School, Escondido, CA**

Glazed Corned Beef

Serves: 4 - 6 *Beef Entreé*

1 package corned beef brisket, with seasonings
$1/2$ cup dark corn syrup
1 tablespoon prepared mustard

Cook corned beef brisket all day in crockpot, covered with water. In small saucepan, combine corn syrup and mustard. Bring to a boil over medium heat, stirring constantly. Reduce heat and simmer, uncovered, 10 minutes, stirring often. Let cool. Trim excess fat from meat and place on rack. Brush top and sides with some of the glaze. Run under broiler 5 to 6" from heat, for 10 minutes, brushing several times with remaining glaze. Note: IF desired, add cabbage and carrots to crockpot for the last hour of cooking.

*"I make this every St. Patrick's Day.
We love it so much I really should prepare it more often!"*

Jan Schulenburg **Irvine High School, Irvine, CA**

Reuben Sandwiches

Serves: 10 *Beef Entreé*

1 2 pound corned beef
butter, as desired
1 loaf dark or light rye bread
1 pound Swiss cheese, sliced
1 (16 ounce) can sauerkraut
Mustard
Thousand Island Dressing (optional)

Place corned beef in small roaster with lid. Be sure to use all of the liquid and seasoning packet. Add water to 2" depth. Cover and place in 300 degree oven for 5 to 8 hours. (I do mine overnight!) Butter bread and grill. Make sandwiches with thinly sliced corned beef piled on rye bread. Top with Swiss cheese, a small amount of well drained sauerkraut and mustard and/or dressing, if desired.

"I make these sandwiches every year for my students. I cut them in quarters so if they don't like them with sauerkraut, I'm not throwing much away. They all taste it and many of them really like it. I then let them make the sandwich anyway they choose."

Sheri Rader   **Chaparral High School, Las Vegas, NV**

Key Lime Pie

Serves: 9 - 12   *Dessert*

    2 cups graham crackers, crushed
    3 tablespoons sugar
    $1/2$ cup butter or margarine, melted
    1 (6 ounce) can frozen lime juice, thawed
    1 (large) container Cool Whip
    1 can Eagle brand milk
    green food coloring

Preheat oven to 350 degrees. Mix together cracker crumbs, sugar and melted butter or margarine; press into bottom of a 9" x 13" dish. Bake 10 minutes; cool. Mix lime juice with Cool Whip and Eagle brand milk. Add food coloring to desired color. Pour into crust and refrigerate 2 hours before serving.

"Great to take anywhere!"

Linda Melton Hayes   **Los Banos High School, Los Banos, CA**

Lucky Leprechaun Cookies

Makes: 15   *Dessert*

    1 package instant pistachio pudding mix
    $1/4$ cup vegetable oil
    1 egg
    $3/4$ cup Bisquick mix

Preheat oven to 350 degrees. Mix ingredients to make a dough. Roll dough into 1" balls. Place on ungreased cookie sheet and gently flatten each cookie. Bake 8 to 10 minutes.

Patty Stroming   **Mitchell Senior Elementary, Atwater, CA**

St. Patrick's Day Parfaits

Serves: 6   *Dessert*

    3 cups miniature marshmallows OR 30 large marshmallows
    $1/2$ cup milk
    1 teaspoon mint extract
    1 cup semi-sweet chocolate chips
    $1/4$ cup powdered sugar
    1 $1/2$ cups heavy whipping cream

Combine marshmallows and milk in medium saucepan; cook over low heat, stirring constantly until marshmallows are melted and mixture is smooth. Place 1 cup mixture in a small bowl; blend in mint extract and set aside. To remaining mixture, add chocolate chips and powdered sugar. Return to low heat and stir until chips are melted. Remove from heat and cool to room temperature. Whip cream until soft peaks form. Fold 1 $1/2$ cups whipped cream into marshmallow-mint mixture. Fold remaining whipped cream into chocolate mixture. Alternately spoon chocolate and mint mixtures into parfait glasses. Chill thoroughly or freeze.

"This dessert and a kiss upon the Blarney Stone makes
St. Patrick's Day a wee bit better!"

Nicole Rehmann   **La Mesa Junior High School, Santa Clarita, CA**

Passover

Passover Rolls

Makes: 10 - 12   ***Breads/Baked Goods***

1 cup water
$^1/_4$ cup sugar
$^1/_2$ cup oil
1 teaspoon salt
2 cups matzah meal
4 eggs

In a saucepan, bring water, sugar, oil and salt to a boil. Pour mixture into large mixing bowl. With wooden spoon or electric mixer, add matzah meal. Mix well, adding one egg at a time. Grease a cookie sheet. Dip hands in water and shape mixture into 10 to 12 rolls. Press a thumbprint into center of each roll. Bake at 375 degrees for 30 to 40 minutes or until lightly browned.

"Soft and tasty treat - great with horseradish or margarine.
A welcome relief from hard matzah."

Susan Eckert   Las Vegas High School, Las Vegas, NV

Spinach Onion Soufflé

Serves: 8   ***Vegetable/Side Dish***

6 tablespoons pareve margarine
4 cups onion, chopped
8 (large) eggs, separated
2 (10 ounce) packages frozen spinach, chopped,
    thawed, squeezed dry
$^1/_3$ cup matzo meal
1 $^1/_2$ teaspoons salt
1 teaspoon garlic powder
$^1/_4$ teaspoon pepper, freshly ground

Melt 4 tablespoons margarine in medium skillet over medium heat; set aside. In another skillet, saute onion and remaining 2 tablespoons margarine; cook until soft and translucent, about 5 minutes. Remove from heat; cool slightly. Heat oven to 350 degrees. Beat egg yolks until thickened. Stir in onions, spinach, matzo meal, salt, garlic powder, pepper and remaining 4 tablespoons melted margarine. Beat egg whites in bowl with electric mixer until stiff peaks form. Thoroughly stir $^1/_4$ of whites into spinach mixture. Fold in remaining whites. Pour into well-greased 2 quart casserole or souffle dish. Bake until browned and set, 40 to 45 minutes.

Karyn Lanham   **Cimarron-Memorial High School, Las Vegas, NV**

Mixed Fruit Cobbler

Serves: 9   *Dessert*

>   3 large eggs
> $^3/_4$ cup + 3 tablespoons sugar
> $^3/_4$ cup matzo meal
> $^1/_4$ cup vegetable oil
>   2 tablespoons potato starch
> $^1/_4$ teaspoon salt
>   8 cups mixed fruit, chopped (peeled, cored apples and pears,
>   blueberries, strawberries or raspberries)
> $^1/_8$ teaspoon ground cinnamon

Preheat oven to 350 degrees. Stir together eggs and $^3/_4$ cup of the sugar in medium bowl until well blended. Add matzo meal, oil, potato starch and salt; mix well. Put fruit in lightly oiled 9" square baking pan. Combine remaining 3 tablespoons sugar with cinnamon in small bowl; sprinkle over fruit. Spoon matzo mixture over fruit, covering as thoroughly as possible. Bake until topping is set and just turning tan, about 45 minutes. Serve hot, warm or at room temperature.

Karyn Lanham   **Cimarron-Memorial High School, Las Vegas, NV**

Easter

Baked Artichoke Squares

Makes: 60   *Appetizers & Beverages*

    2 (8 ounce) cans Pillsbury crescent dinner rolls
    1 (14 ounce) can artichoke hearts, drained, chopped
    1 (9 ounce) package frozen spinach, thawed
    3/4 cup Parmesan cheese, grated
    2/3 cup mayonnaise
    2/3 cup sour cream
    1/8 teaspoon garlic powder

Heat oven to 375 degrees. Roll dough into 4 long rectangles. Place
crosswise in ungreased 15" x 10" x 1" baking pan; press over bottom and 1"
up sides to form a crust. Press perforations to seal. Bake 10 to 12 minutes
or until lightly golden brown. In medium bowl, combine all remaining
ingredients, mixing well. Spread mixture evenly over partially baked crust.
Bake an additional 8 to 10 minutes or until topping is thoroughly heated.
Cut into 1 1/2" squares. Serve warm. Note: This can be made ahead. Bake
crust, assemble mixture and refrigerate. Just before serving, top with
mixture and bake 5 to 10 minutes.

Deborah L. Weiss   **Ayala High School, Chino Hills, CA**

Deviled Eggs

Makes: 24   *Appetizers & Beverages*

    12 eggs, hard cooked
    1/3 cup mayonnaise or sour cream
    1 tablespoon vinegar
    1/2 teaspoon Worcestershire sauce
    1 teaspoon prepared mustard
    1/4 teaspoon salt
    1/4 teaspoon onion powder
    dash ground white pepper
    Garnishes: paprika, sliced black olives, tiny shrimp, chopped parsley

Remove shells from eggs and halve lengthwise. Carefully remove yolks and
place in a medium bowl. Mash yolks with a fork until smooth. Stir in
remaining ingredients; mix well. Lightly spoon mixture back into egg white
halves or pipe the filling through a pastry bag (or Ziploc bag with one

corner cut out). Refrigerate until ready to serve. Garnish as desired.

*"I have used this recipe with students grades 7 through 12.
They truly enjoy the taste! Bon Apetit!"*

Martha Bradshaw   **Lakewood High School, Lakewood, CA**

Salmon Mousse

Serves: 6 - 8   *Appetizers & Beverages*

1 package gelatin
$1/4$ cup hot water
1 (16 ounce) can salmon, with liquid
$1/2$ cup celery, diced
$1/4$ cup green pepper, minced
$1/4$ cup pimento or sweet red pepper, chopped
$3/4$ cup margarine
2 teaspoons onion, grated
$1/8$ teaspoon pepper

Spray a 1 quart mold with nonstick cooking spray; set aside. Soften gelatin in hot water; cool. In food processor, place all ingredients and process until blended. Pour into prepared mold. Refrigerate until set. Remove by dipping mold into warm water, then invert onto serving platter. Serve with crackers.

Gloria Francuch   **Carpinteria High School, Carpinteria, CA**

French Toast for a Spring Brunch

Serves: 10 - 12   *Breads/Baked Goods*

1 cup brown sugar
$1/2$ cup butter, melted
3 teaspoons cinnamon, divided
3 tart apples, peeled, sliced
$1/2$ cup dried cranberries
1 loaf French bread, (not sourdough), cut into 1" slices
6 eggs
1 $1/2$ cups milk
1 tablespoon vanilla

Combine brown sugar, butter, 1 teaspoon cinnamon in a 9" x 13" baking dish. Add apples and cranberries. Toss and coat, then spread mixture evenly over bottom of pan. Arrange bread slices on top. Mix together eggs, milk, vanilla and remaining cinnamon and pour over bread. Cover and refrigerate 4 to 24 hours. Bake, covered, at 375 degrees for 40 minutes. Uncover and bake an additional 5 minutes. Let stand 5 minutes, then serve warm.

"It's easy and delicious!"

Betty Rabin-Fung   **Sierra Vista Junior High School, Santa Clarita, CA**

Soft Pretzel "Prize"

Makes: 12   *Breads/Baked Goods*

1 $1/3$ cups warm water
1 package dry yeast
3 $1/2$ to 4 cups flour
$1/2$ teaspoon salt
1 tablespoon sugar
1 egg, mixed with 1 tablespoon water
kosher salt

Pour warm water into large bowl; sprinkle yeast on top and stir. Add 1 cup of flour, salt and sugar to yeast; mix. Add remaining flour, 1 cup at a time. Knead dough 5 to 7 minutes. Preheat oven to 400 degrees. Cut dough in half. Cut each half into 6 equal pieces. Roll each piece into a 12" to 15" rope. Shape into pretzel. Brush with egg mixture and sprinkle on kosher salt. Bake 15 minutes.

"Pretzels come from the word PRETIOLA, which means PRIZE. Priests used to give these to students who learned their Bible lessons correctly."

Gaylen Roe   **Magnolia Junior High School, Chino, CA**

Bird Seed Salad

Serves: 8 - 10   *Salad*

1 (small) head red cabbage, chopped
1 (small) head white cabbage, chopped
3 green onions, chopped
1 (large) can Mandarin oranges, drained
2 tablespoons sesame seeds
$1/4$ cup almonds, sliced
1 package Oriental Top Ramen noodles, crushed
Dressing:
$1/4$ cup olive oil
$1/3$ cup rice vinegar
seasoning packet from Top Ramen
salt and pepper, to taste

In large bowl, combine chopped cabbage, onions, orange segments, sesame seeds, almonds and ramen noodles. Blend dressing ingredients and pour over salad. Toss and serve.

"My family enjoys this recipe as a summer meal with a bit of cooked chicken added to the salad."

Marleigh Williams   **Corning High School, Corning, CA**

Spring Ambrosia

Serves: 10 - 12   *Salad*

16 ounces cream cheese
1 can crushed pineapple
1 (small) can Mandarin orange slices
1 cup coconut
1 cup colored miniature marshmallows

Soften cream cheese. Stir in crushed pineapple, orange slices (reserve several for garnish), coconut and marshmallows. Mix gently and spread in glass dish. Garnish with orange slices in the shape of a bunny or a cross. Chill in refrigerator overnight.

"This is a five generation family recipe, loved by all who try it!"

Georgette Phillips   **Silverado High School, Victorville, CA**

The "Eyes" Have It Salad

Serves: 8   *Salad*

1 tablespoon olive oil
2 (8.5 ounce) cans artichoke hearts, drained
2 cups (canned) black-eyed peas, drained, rinsed
6 ounces part-skim cheese, cubed
1 cup celery, sliced
$3/4$ cup red onion, finely diced
$1/2$ (6 ounce) jar roasted bell pepper (reserve juice),
    cut into $1/4$" squares
3 to 4 tablespoons Italian dressing
salt and pepper, to taste
Bibb lettuce leaves

Heat olive oil in large skillet over medium heat until hot. Add artichoke hearts; cook 5 to 7 minutes or until tender and lightly browned. Remove from pan, cool and place in large bowl. Add peas, cheese, celery, onion, red peppers and 1 tablespoon of reserved juice from peppers in bowl with artichokes. Pour Italian dressing over mixture; toss lightly. Cover and refrigerate 4 hours. Toss 2 more times. Taste and season with salt and pepper. Serve chilled over lettuce leaves.

Teresa Stahl   **Needles High School, Needles, CA**

Pepperoni Green Beans

Serves: 8 – 10   *Vegetable/Side Dish*

olive oil
1 (small) onion, diced
2 cloves garlic, minced
1 can whole tomatoes
2 pounds green beans, fresh, cut into bite-sized pieces
2 sticks pepperoni, diced

Place a little olive oil in a pan to cover the bottom. Saute onion and garlic until tender. Add tomatoes, green beans and pepperoni; cook until tender.

Marci Yarmon   **Granite Hills High School, San Diego, CA**

California Quiche

Serves: 8   *Chicken Entreé*

1 pre-made pie crust, unbaked
$3/4$ pound sweet Italian turkey sausage
3 eggs, slightly beaten
1 $3/4$ cup hot milk
$1/4$ cup chopped green chiles
2 cups Monterey jack cheese, grated
nonstick cooking spray

Line a quiche dish or deep dish pie pan with ready made pie crust; set aside. Preheat oven to 400 degrees. Remove sausage from casing. Spray a nonstick frying pan with nonstick cooking spray. Break up sausage and cook at medium heat until completely browned; drain off fat and spoon sausage into pie crust. In bowl, combine eggs, milk, chiles and cheese. Pour over sausage. Bake 25 to 30 minutes until center is firm. Serve warm.

"We serve this on every holiday that our kids wake up early.
It's perfect for breakfast or brunch, but tastes best as a leftover!
Our family likes to call it Cali-fornia Quiche!"

Mary Jo Cali   **Arroyo Grande High School, Arroyo Grande, CA**

Easter Breakfast Bake

Serves: 12   *Pork Entreé*

- 2 pounds bulk pork sausage
- 3/4 cup broccoli florets
- 1/2 cup green pepper
- 1 cup asparagus, cut into small pieces
- 1/2 cup red onion,
- 3 cups jack cheese, shredded
- 12 slices white bread, cubed
- 12 eggs
- 2 cups milk
- 1 teaspoon salt
- 1 teaspoon pepper
- 2 teaspoons dry mustard

Preheat oven to 350 degrees. Cook sausage until browned and crumbly; drain all but 2 tablespoons grease, set sausage aside. Chop vegetables and saute in reserved grease; drain. Mix cooked sausage with vegetables and cheese. Layer bread and cheese mixture in a 9" x 13" pan. Combine eggs, milk and spices in large bowl; beat until light. Pour egg mixture over layered ingredients. Bake 1 1/2 hours.

"Great for Easter brunch or anytime you want to serve guests breakfast."

Donna Young   Santa Maria High School, Santa Maria, CA

Ham with Raisin Cranberry Sauce

Serves: 6   *Pork Entreé*

- whole cloves, as desired
- dash salt
- 1/2 cup brown sugar
- 2 tablespoons corn starch
- dash ground cloves
- 1 1/2 cups cranberry juice cocktail
- 1/2 cup orange juice
- 1/2 cup raisins
- baked ham

In saucepan, mix whole cloves, salt, brown sugar, corn starch and ground cloves together. Stir in fruit juices and raisins. Cook and stir until mixture is thick and boiling. Spoon part of the sauce over ham and bake 20 minutes, adding more sauce, if necessary. Pass remaining sauce with cooked ham when serving.

Janet Tingley   Atascadero High School, Atascadero, CA

Alicia's Easter Bunny Cake

Serves: 8   ***Dessert***

Cake:
2 cups all-purpose flour
1 1/2 cups sugar
1 tablespoon baking powder
1 teaspoon salt
1 cup milk
1/2 cup shortening
2 teaspoons vanilla
4 egg whites
Frosting:
1 pound confectioner's sugar
1/4 teaspoon salt
1 teaspoon vanilla
2/3 stick butter, softened
milk, as needed
assorted food colorings
decorations

Preheat oven to 350 degrees. Cake: Grease and lightly flour two 8" or 9" round baking pans. In a mixing bowl, stir together flour, sugar, baking powder and salt. Add milk, shortening and vanilla to flour mixture; beat with electric mixer on low speed until combined. Beat on medium speed for 2 minutes. Add unbeaten egg whites; beat on medium speed for 2 minutes more, scraping sides of bowl frequently. Turn into prepared pans; spread evenly. Bake 25 to 30 minutes for all cake sizes or until a toothpick is inserted and comes out clean. Cool 10 minutes on wire racks. Remove and cool completely before frosting. Meanwhile, prepare frosting: Combine frosting ingredients in a large bowl and beat with electric mixer until smooth and creamy. If too stiff, add a few drops of milk to thin.

Assemble cake: Use a large platter or foil covered cardboard piece for base. Place one full layer in center of base to form bunny head. Cut the other layer into three pieces; two equal half circles from each side to form ears. Place at the top of the head. Use the remaining center piece for a collar at the bottom of bunny's head.

> *"I've made this for my family since I was a teenager.*
> *It can double as a birthday cake!"*

Alicia Pucci   **Kenilworth Junior High School, Petaluma, CA**

Caramel Apple Cake

Serves: 6   ***Dessert***

   1 ¹/2 cups Bisquick
   ²/3 cup granulated sugar
   ¹/2 cup milk
   2 (medium) cooking apples, peeled, sliced
   1 tablespoon lemon juice
   ³/4 cup brown sugar, packed
   1/ teaspoon cinnamon
   1 cup water, boiling

Preheat oven to 350 degrees. Mix Bisquick and sugar in a medium sized
bowl; beat in milk until blended. Pour into ungreased square 9" x 9" x 2"
pan. Top with apples; sprinkle with lemon juice. In small bowl, combine
brown sugar with cinnamon and sprinkle over apples. Pour boiling water
over top and bake 50 to 60 minutes, until toothpick inserted in center
comes out clean. Serve warm.

> *"A student made this during a "free lab" and everyone loved it!*
> *Great for Easter morning."*

Wendy Duncan   **West Covina High School, West Covina, CA**

Easter Basket Cupcakes

Makes: 33   ***Dessert***

   2 cups sugar
   1 ³/4 cup all-purpose flour
   ³/4 cup Hershey's Cocoa or Hershey's Dutch Processed Cocoa
   1 ¹/2 teaspoons baking powder
   1 ¹/2 teaspoons baking soda
   1 teaspoon salt
   2 eggs
   1 cup milk
   ¹/2 cup vegetable oil
   2 teaspoons vanilla
   1 cup boiling water
   1 (16 ounce) can cream vanilla ready-to-spread frosting
   3 ³/4 cups (10 ounce package) Mounds Sweetened
        Coconut flakes, tinted green
   Assorted Hershey's Easter candies
        (Jolly Rancher Jolly Beans, Jellybeans, Cadbury's Mini Eggs Candy,
        Hershey's Candy-Coated Eggs, Hershey's Mini Robin Eggs,
        Hershey's Kisses Milk Chocolates)
   33 Twizzlers Strawberry Twists

> ***Photo on***
> ***opposite page***

Heat oven to 350 degrees. Line muffin cups with paper bake cups. Stir
together sugar, flour, cocoa, baking powder, baking soda and salt in large
bowl. Add eggs, milk, oil and vanilla; beat on medium speed of electric

mixer 2 minutes. Stir in boiling water (batter will be thin). Fill muffin cups ²/₃ full. Bake 22 to 25 minutes or until wooden pick inserted in center comes out clean. Cool completely. To make Easter baskets, frost each cupcake with vanilla frosting. Immediately make "nest" on top of each cupcake with tinted coconut; place assorted candies in nests. For handle, insert wooden pick in each end of strawberry twists; press down into each side of each cupcake, bending to form handle.

Hershey Foods   **Hershey, PA**

Easter Bird Nests

Makes: 20   ***Dessert***

   1 (12 ounce) package milk chocolate chips
   1 (12 ounce) package semi-sweet chocolate chips
   1 (8 ounce) package coconut, shredded
   1 bag jelly beans

Prepare a double boiler with water below and bring to a boil. Reduce heat and add insert on top. Pour chocolate chips into double boiler and stir, over medium-low heat until melted. Add coconut, 4 ounces at a time, and stir to combine. Cool slightly, then shape into 3" pancakes onto waxed paper. Make a dent in center with your thumb. Arrange three jelly beans in center of each. Allow to cool on waxed paper or chill in refrigerator.

"Thanks to my Aunt Joanne, for her wonderful recipe. Students love this easy recipe."

Patti Bartholomew   **Casa Roble High School, Orangevale, CA**

Easter Bunny Cake

Makes: 2 bunny cakes   ***Dessert***

   1 box cake mix
   2 cans frosting, divided
   coconut
   jelly beans

Prepare cake mix according to package directions. Pour into 2 round 8" or 9" layer pans. Bake according to package directions. Remove from oven, cool 10 minutes, then remove from pans to cool completely. For first bunny, cut one layer in half. Put halves together with frosting. Stand cake upright on cut edge. With sharp knife, cut a V-notch about a third of the way up the semi-circle. Use the cake notched cut out pieces to attach with toothpicks for the tail. The area below notch will form bunny's head. The ²/₃ area above the notch will shape the bunny's rounded back. Frost with remaining frosting from first can. Sprinkle generously with coconut. Use jelly beans for eyes and nose. Make ears out of construction paper and place in head. Follow same procedure using second cake layer for second bunny.

"Makes two table decorations that are adorable and tasty!"

Sharon Chavez   **Rogers Middle School, Long Beach, CA**

Leche Flan

Serves: 10   *Dessert*

  1 cup sugar, divided
  12 egg yolks
  1 can evaporated milk
  1 teaspoon vanilla
  1/4 teaspoon lemon rind, grated

Preheat oven to 325 degrees. Over low heat, melt 1/3 cup sugar in an 8" round baking pan. Tip pan back and forth to distribute caramelized sugar evenly and avoid burning (which can happen suddenly). Beat egg yolks until well blended. Gradually add remaining 2/3 cup sugar; mix thoroughly. Pour milk slowly into yolk/sugar mixture. Add vanilla and lemon rind; mix thoroughly. Pour into caramel-lined pan. Place in a larger, shallow baking pan and set in center of oven. Pour hot water into larger pan to come halfway up sides of 8" pan. Bake 1 1/2 to 2 hours, or until knife inserted in center comes out clean. Chill, covered, for several hours or overnight before serving. To unmold, loosen sides with a knife. Quickly turn pan over onto serving plate.

  "This is a favorite Filipino family dessert, thanks to Lola!"
Beth Pool   **Chaboya Middle School, San Jose, CA**

Mounds Coconut Easter Basket Cake

Serves: 8   *Dessert*

  1 package white cake mix with pudding
  2 cups Mounds Sweetened Coconut Flakes, divided
  1/3 cup butter, softened
  3 1/2 cups powdered sugar
  1 teaspoon vanilla
  3 tablespoons milk

Photo opposite page 96

Prepare cake batter with whole eggs as directed on package; stir in 1/2 cup coconut and bake in (2) 9" round cake pans. Bake and cool as directed. While cake is baking, prepare frosting: Beat butter in medium bowl with 1 cup powdered sugar and vanilla; add 2 1/2 cups powdered sugar alternately with milk until desired spreading consistency is reached; set aside. Place 1 layer on serving plate, bottom side up; frost top layer. Place second layer on top, top side up. Frost sides. Mark a 6" circle from center of top layer. Using fork, gently remove small amount of cake from within circle, forming an indentation to allow basket to be filled. Lightly frost edges of top. Cut lightweight cardboard into 14" x 3/4" wide strip for handle; cover with plastic wrap. Bend and insert handle ends into top of cake about 1" from sides; frost. Decorate with jelly beans and single licorice strands. When frosting on sides of cake is firm, with fork, alternately press fork tines vertically, and horizontally, forming basket pattern. Combine 3 drops green food color with 3/4 teaspoon water; add to remaining 1 1/2 cups coconut; stir until evenly tinted. Use immediately. Place coconut "grass" on top and
98

decorate with Hershey's Mini Kisses Chocolate and assorted candies. Separate licorice into 3 strand groups; twist and place around top rim. Place jelly beans around bottom. Remove handle before serving.

Hershey Foods   **Hershey, PA**

Quick Citrus Cookies

Makes: 2 ¹/₂ dozen   *Dessert*

1 (12 ounce) box Nilla vanilla wafers
1 (6 ounce) can frozen orange juice concentrate, thawed
¹/₂ cup margarine, softened
1 (1 pound) box powdered sugar
coconut or ground nuts

Crush vanilla wafers using a rolling pin. Mix the crumbs with orange juice, margarine and powdered sugar, using an electric mixer. The mixture will be very stiff. Shape mixture into 1" balls and roll in either coconut or ground nuts.

"Thanks to my cousin, Charlene, for this quick, easy recipe!"

Carole Delap   **Golden West High School, Visalia, CA**

Strawberry Cheese Pie with Pecan Pie Crust

Makes: 2 pies   *Dessert*

¹/₄ cup brown sugar
1 stick butter
1 cup flour
1 cup pecans, broken
Filling:
1 (small) box strawberry gelatin
1 cup boiling water
1 cup sugar
8 ounces cream cheese
1 teaspoon vanilla
1 (large) can Pet milk, chilled, whipped
fresh strawberries, cleaned, hulled

Preheat oven to 250 degrees. Mix together brown sugar, butter, flour and pecans. Pat out thinly onto cookie sheet and bake 15 minutes. Remove from oven and crumble into two pie pans to form crust. Dissolve gelatin in boiling water; cool. Cream sugar and cream cheese, adding vanilla and cooled gelatin; mix well and fold into whipped milk. Pour into prepared pie shells. Carefully place whole strawberries in pie. Chill and serve same day.

Judy Dobkins   **Redlands High School, Redlands, CA**

Yellow Jello ✓

Serves: 8   *Dessert*

2 (3 ounce) packages lemon jello
2 cups hot water
2 cups 7-Up
2 bananas, peeled, sliced
1 (large) can crushed pineapple
1 egg
1 $1/2$ tablespoons flour
$1/2$ cup sugar
1 cup whipped cream

Mix jello, hot water and 7-Up together; stir until dissolved. Add sliced bananas and pineapple. Pour into mold or rectangular glass casserole. Chill until firm. Mix egg with flour and sugar in top of double boiler. Cook over boiling water until thickened; cool. Fold in whipped cream. Spread over congealed jello.

"Granny always served this cool salad with her Easter ham dinner."

DeLisa Davis   **Sutter High School, Sutter, CA**

Cinco de Mayo

Acapulco Dip ✓

Serves: 10-12 *Appetizers & Beverages*

2 (8 ounce) packages cream cheese, cubed
1 (large) avocado, peeled, pitted, cubed
1 jar Herdez salsa
2 cups cheddar cheese, grated
1 jar olives, sliced
6 green onions, chopped
tortilla chips, for serving

In a microwave safe 9" x 9" dish, layer ingredients in order listed. Heat in microwave on HIGH 10 minutes, turning dish halfway through the cooking. Serve with tortilla chips.

"This recipe is always a big hit at potlucks. We make this in class, and the students love it too!"

Mary Nafis **Montclair High School, Montclair, CA**

California Bean Dip ✓

Serves: 8 - 10 *Appetizers & Beverages*

2 cans black beans, drained
$3/4$ cup Monterey Jack cheese, shredded
✓ 1 bunch fresh cilantro, washed
1 (12 ounce) container sour cream
1 (12 ounce) container guacamole
2 (medium) tomatoes, chopped
1 (small) can black olives, chopped
1 bunch green onions, chopped
Tortilla chips

Preheat oven to 350 degrees. In a large glass casserole dish, place drained beans. Top with shredded cheese and bake until cheese melts. Pinch off leaves from cilantro and sprinkle over cheese. Spread sour cream and guacamole over. Sprinkle with tomatoes, olives and onions. Refrigerate 1 hour. Serve with tortilla chips.

"Great for Super Bowl or Cinco de Mayo!"

Donna Abbey **Crescenta Valley High School, La Crescenta, CA**

Green Avocado Salsa

Serves: 6 - 8   *Appetizers & Beverages*

2 avocados
1 lime, juiced
3 tablespoons lemon juice
3 green onions, finely chopped
1 white onion, peeled, diced
5 tomatillos, peeled, seeded, finely chopped
$1/4$ cup roasted green chiles, chopped
1 tablespoon garlic, peeled finely minced
salt and pepper to taste.

Peel, seed and cube avocado into $1/4$" cubes. Immediately cover with lime and lemon juice in a bowl to avoid turning brown. Gently toss with remaining ingredients and garnish with a curl of lemon or lime peel.

"Great for demonstrations and fun to do in any
Foods, Nutrition, comprehensive or culinary program."

Priscilla Burns   **Pleasant Valley High School, Chico, CA**

Mango Salsa Guacamole

Makes: 2 cups   *Appetizers & Beverages*

1 cup cherry tomatoes, assorted colors look best
1 lime, juiced
$1/2$ bunch cilantro
1 (small) green chile, seeded, deveined
1 teaspoon vinegar
dash Angostura bitters (optional)
salt and pepper, to taste
1 mango, peeled, seeded, cut into $1/2$" cubes
1 to 2 avocados, peeled, seeded, cut into $1/2$" cubes
Tabasco sauce, to taste
Tortilla chips, for serving

In a food processor, pulse the tomatoes 1 or 2 times or until coarsely chopped. Add lime juice, cilantro and chile; pulse a few more times until cilantro is coarsely chopped. Pour into a bowl and stir in remaining ingredients. Add Tabasco if more spice is desired and serve with tortilla chips.

"This salsa-guacamole is delicious served over chicken, pork or fish."

Larkin Evans   **Half Moon Bay High School, Half Moon Bay, CA**

Mexican Shrimp Cocktail

Serves: 4   *Appetizers & Beverages*

3 tomatoes, finely diced
2 green onions, thinly sliced
1 (small) clove garlic, minced
1 tablespoon cilantro, chopped
1 tablespoon fresh lemon juice
1 tablespoon fresh lime juice
1 teaspoon salt
$1/2$ teaspoon black pepper
$1/2$ pound shrimp, cooked
1 avocado, peeled, diced
lime wedges

Stir together tomatoes, green onion, garlic, cilantro, lemon and lime juice, salt and pepper. Add shrimp to salsa, cover and marinate at least 1 hour. Just before serving, remove shrimp and stir in finely diced avocado. Spoon salsa into 4 serving dishes and arrange shrimp and lime on top.

Debbie Dodson   Paradise High School, Paradise, CA

Party Nachos ✓

Serves: a crowd   *Appetizers & Beverages*

1 $1/2$ cups lean ground meat
1 (large) onion, diced
1 (30 ounce) can refried beans
1 (7 ounce) can diced green chiles
2 cups Monterey jack cheese, grated
2 cups cheddar cheese, grated
1 bottle green chile salsa
$1/2$ cup green onions, chopped
1 cup black olives, sliced
1 cup sour cream
1 avocado, peeled, seeded, diced
tortilla chips

Preheat oven to 375 degrees. Brown ground meat with onions; drain excess grease. Spread refried beans in bottom of a 10" x 15" oven proof serving dish. Spread browned meat on top of beans. Sprinkle chiles and cheese over meat. Drizzle green chile salsa over all. Bake about 25 minutes. Remove from oven and top with green onions and olives. Place mounds of sour cream and avocado on top just before serving. Serve warm with tortilla chips.

Laurie Owen   Challenger Middle School, San Diego, CA

Sopes

Makes: 16   *Appetizers & Beverages*

2 cups masa harina flour
$1/4$ cup lard or shortening
1 $1/4$ cups warm water
small amount of oil, for frying
1 $3/4$ cups refried beans, warmed
1 cup cheddar, Monterey jack, or cotija cheese, shredded
   or crumbled
Optional toppings: chopped tomato, sour cream, olives, salsa,
   jalapeño peppers

Cut shortening into flour with a pastry blender until mixture resembles coarse crumbs. Gradually add water, kneading dough until smooth. Form dough into 16 small balls. Pat each ball into a 3" patty; rest on waxed paper. Heat a small amount of oil in large skillet over medium-high heat for 1 to 2 minutes. Cook patties 3 minutes on each side or until golden brown; adding oil as needed. Top with beans, cheese and preferred toppings.

Joye Cantrell   **Rialto High School, Rialto, CA**

Tortilla Soup

Serves: 6   *Soups*

1 cup onion, diced
1 tablespoon oil
1 (4 ounce) can diced green chiles
1 package taco seasoning
2 $1/2$ cups chopped tomatoes, pureed
6 cups chicken broth
2 cups corn, frozen
2 cups chicken or turkey, cooked, diced
$1/3$ cup cilantro, chopped
tortilla chips
Monterey jack cheese, shredded

In large saucepan, over medium heat, saute onion in oil 3 to 4 minutes. Stir in chiles and taco seasoning mix; cook 1 minute. Add tomatoes and chicken broth. Bring to a boil. Add corn and chicken or turkey, reduce heat and simmer 5 minutes. Add cilantro. Serve with broken tortilla chips and top with shredded cheese.

"I get rave reviews whenever this soup is served!"

Carol Steele   **Arroyo Seco Junior High School, Valencia, CA**

Easy Fiesta Rice

Serves: 4 - 6   *Vegetable/Side Dish*

1 (14.5 ounce) can stewed tomatoes (with onion and green pepper)
1 1/2 cups chicken broth
1 1/4 cups white rice, uncooked
1 tablespoon butter or margarine
2 teaspoon chili powder
3/4 teaspoon oregano
1/2 teaspoon garlic salt

In a medium saucepan, combine all ingredients. Bring to a boil. Reduce heat; cover and simmer 25 minutes. Fluff with a fork and serve.

Cindy Peters   **Black Diamond Middle School, Antioch, CA**

Chicken Acapulco

Serves: 4   *Chicken Entreé*

4 whole chicken breasts
3 tablespoons butter
3 tablespoons flour
1 cup sour cream
1 can cream of chicken soup
2 ounces diced green chiles
1/2 teaspoon onion salt
2 cups Monterey jack cheese, shredded

Preheat oven to 350 degrees. Place chicken in an oblong pan. In a saucepan, melt butter; stir in flour until smooth. Add sour cream, stirring until blended and starting to bubble, being careful not to boil. Add soup, chiles and onion salt, stirring until blended. Pour over chicken. Bake 30 minutes. Sprinkle cheese over top and bake 10 minutes more.

"My dear friend, Liane Daniels, prepared this for our Book Club meeting. This is really delicious!"

Linda Heinbach   **Yosemite High School, Oakhurst, CA**

Taco Two-Zies

Photo opposite page 97

Serves: 10   *Beef Entreé*

1 pound ground beef
2 (1 ounce) packages Lawry's Taco Spices & Seasonings
3/4 cup water
1 (1 pound 14 ounce) can refried beans, warmed
10 (small) flour tortillas (fajita size), warmed
10 (jumbo) taco shells, heated according to package directions
Taco toppings: Shredded lettuce, cheddar cheese
      and chopped tomatoes

In large skillet, brown ground beef over medium heat until crumbly; drain fat. Stir in 1 package Taco Spices & Seasonings and water; bring to a boil. Reduce heat to low and cook, uncovered, 10 minutes, stirring occasionally. In medium bowl mix together beans and remaining package Taco Spices & Seasonings. Spread about $1/3$ cup seasoned beans all the way to the edge of each flour tortilla. Place a taco shell on center of each bean filled tortilla and fold edges up around shell, lightly pressing to stick tortilla to shell. Fill each taco with about 3 tablespoons taco meat. Top with your choice of taco toppings.

Lawry's Foods, Inc.   **Monrovia, CA**

Chili Verde Burritos

Serves: 4 - 6   *Pork Entreé*

   $1/4$ pound pork, cubed
   1 package pork gravy mix
   1 cup cold water
   $1/4$ cup diced green chiles
   $1/2$ cup salsa
   6 flour tortillas

Cut pork into small cubes; fry until browned. Add remaining ingredients, except tortillas. Simmer 10 minutes or until the sauce thickens. Serve on warmed tortillas.

"This is a popular lab during our meat unit."

LeeAnn Bitner   **Alta High School, Sandy, UT**

Spicy Triangle Tostada

> **Photo opposite page 97**

Makes: 8   *Pork Entreé*

   2 (large) flour tortillas, burrito size
   vegetable oil
   1 pound lean ground pork
   1 (1 ounce) package Lawry's Hot Taco Spices & Seasonings
   $2/3$ cup water
   1 (16 ounce) can refried beans, warmed
   Toppings: Shredded lettuce and cheese, chopped tomatoes

Preheat oven to 400 degrees. Cut each tortilla into quarters, forming 4 triangles. Place triangles in a single layer on baking sheet. Brush each side of triangle lightly with oil. Bake 4 to 5 minutes or until golden brown and crispy; let cool. Meanwhile, in large skillet, brown ground pork over medium high heat until crumbly; drain fat. Stir in Hot Taco Spices & Seasonings and water. Bring to a boil; reduce heat to low and cook, uncovered for 7 minutes, stirring occasionally. To assemble tostadas, evenly divide and spread refried beans on each tortilla triangle. Spread about $1/4$ cup seasoned pork on top of beans. Top with shredded lettuce and cheese and tomatoes, as desired.

Lawry's Foods, Inc.   **Monrovia, CA**

Chilaquiles

Serves: 4 *Meatless Entreé*

2 pasilla chiles
1 clove garlic, minced
1/2 teaspoon oregano
3/4 teaspoon Knorr chicken flavored bouillon
1/2 onion, minced
15 to 20 corn tortillas
oil, for frying
1 cup cheese, shredded
1/2 onion, sliced

Boil chiles in small amount of water until soft. Blend chile with garlic, oregano, chicken bouillon and onion; set aside. Cut tortillas into strips; fry in a small amount of oil until crisp. Pour blended chile mixture over tortillas, top with cheese and sliced onions. Cover and simmer until cheese melts.

"This recipe was given to me by my neighbor, Maria Vera. She said in Mexico the dish is often served for breakfast with a fried egg on top."

Diane Castro **Temecula Valley High School, Temecula, CA**

Tropical Fruit Paletas

Serves: 8 *Dessert*

1 1/2 papaya or mango, peeled, seeded, pureed
1/2 cup water
2 1/2 cups sugar
1 tablespoon lime juice
8 plastic molds or paper cups with wooden sticks

In a medium sized bowl, combine pureed fruit with water, sugar and lime juice. Taste mixture and add sugar and/or lime juice to taste. (When frozen, flavors will be muted, so try for a slightly sweeter or tarter flavor.) Stir mixture until sugar is dissolved completely. Fill molds or cups, leaving 1/4" space at top to allow for expansion. Set mold lids in place and insert wooden sticks. Freeze until firm, approximately 2 hours. Rinse under warm water to dislodge. Serve and enjoy!

Yolanda Carlos **Victor Valley High School, Victorville, CA**

Mother's Day & Father's Day

Sake-Garlic Shrimp

Serves: 4   *Appetizers & Beverages*

  1 teaspoon garlic, minced
  1 teaspoon shallot, minced
  1 teaspoon olive oil
  10 ounces shrimp, peeled, deveined
  $1/2$ cup sake
  2 tablespoons butter
  1 tablespoon soy sauce
  1 teaspoon fresh parsley, chopped

Using a 10" saute pan over medium heat, stir garlic, shallot and oil until golden brown, about 2 minutes. Next, add shrimp and sake. Cook until shrimp are opaque but still moist-looking at the thickest part, 3 to 5 minutes. Add butter, soy sauce and parsley. Stir until butter is melted and sauce is blended.

"This is one of my husband's favorite recipes. We enjoy it as an appetizer, without the sauce. It is also fantastic as an entree, served over pasta."

Delaine Smith   **West Valley High School, Cottonwood, CA**

Almond Struesel Tea Ring

Makes: 1 ring   *Breads/Baked Goods*

Dough:
2 packages active dry yeast
$3/4$ cup warm water (110 to 115 degrees)
$3/4$ cup warm milk (110 to 115 degrees)
$1/4$ cup butter or margarine, softened
$1/2$ cup sugar
2 eggs
1 teaspoon salt
5 $1/4$ to 5 $1/2$ cups all-purpose flour
Filling:
$1/2$ cup almond paste
$1/4$ cup butter or margarine, softened
$1/2$ cup brown sugar, packed
$1/4$ teaspoon almond extract
Topping:
3 tablespoons sugar
1 tablespoon all-purpose flour
1 tablespoon butter or margarine, softened
Icing:
1 $1/2$ cups powdered sugar
1 to 2 tablespoons milk
$1/4$ teaspoon almond extract

Dough: In a mixing bowl, dissolve yeast in warm water; set stand 5 minutes. Add milk, butter, sugar, eggs and salt; mix well. Add 2 cups flour; beat until smooth. Stir in enough remaining flour to form a soft dough. Turn onto a floured surface; knead until smooth and elastic, about 6 to 8 minutes. Place in a greased bowl, turning once to grease top. Cover and let rise in warm place until doubled in size, about 1 hour. Meanwhile, prepare remaining ingredients. In a mixing bowl, beat filling ingredients until smooth; set aside. Combine topping ingredients (mixture will be crumbly); set aside. Beat together icing ingredients until smooth; set aside. Punch dough down, roll out to a 15" x 10" rectangle. Spread filling ingredients over dough. Roll up jelly roll style. Grease a large cookie sheet. form a ring with dough, connecting the two ends; seal seams. Slice diagonally about halfway down every 3" to 4". Cover and let rise in a warm place until doubled, about 30 minutes. Sprinkle topping ingredients over ring and bake at 350 degrees for 35 to 40 minutes, or until golden brown. Cool on wire rack. Drizzle icing over ring and serve. Note: You may also choose to bake the dough like cinnamon rolls. Roll the dough jelly roll style, but cut into 12 slices and bake in a 9" x 13" pan.

"This recipe was given to me by my mother.
It is a great way to spoil your loved ones!"

Anita Cornwall   **Cimarron-Memorial High School, Las Vegas, NV**

Whole Wheat Belgium Waffles

Makes: 4 - 5 *Breads/Baked Goods*

2 eggs
1 $^1/_4$ cups milk
5 tablespoons oil
1 $^1/_2$ cups whole wheat flour
$^3/_4$ teaspoon salt
2 teaspoons baking powder
3 tablespoons sugar

Mix eggs with milk and oil until light and fluffy. Sift dry ingredients together and fold into milk mixture, just until mixed. Bake in hot waffle iron. Serve with fresh fruit and cream, syrup, powdered sugar or butter and jam.

"My 20 year old son won't eat any other waffles. No other recipe even compares to these - delicious for breakfast or lunch."

Carol Winter **Hillcrest High School, Midvale, UT**

Mandarin Orange Delight

Serves: 12 *Salad*

1 ($^3/_4$ ounce) package tapioca pudding
1 (3 ounce) package lemon pudding
3 cups hot water
1 (3 ounce) package orange jello
1 pint whipping cream
2 teaspoons vanilla
$^1/_4$ cup powdered sugar
1 can mandarin oranges, drained
1 (8 ounce) can crushed pineapple, drained

Stir tapioca and lemon puddings into hot water. Bring to a boil; remove from heat and stir in orange jello, until dissolved. Cool. Beat whipping cream with vanilla and powdered sugar until stiff peaks form. Fold into pudding mixture. Fold in fruit. Chill until set. Pour into a mold or 9" x 13" pan. Garnish as desired.

"Canned diced apricots may be substituted for the Mandarin oranges."

Mary Lash **Paramount High School, Paramount, CA**

Pear and Gorgonzola Salad

Serves: 6 *Salad*

    1 cup walnut halves
    2 tablespoons balsamic vinegar
    $1/4$ teaspoon salt
    $1/4$ teaspoon Dijon mustard
    6 tablespoons extra-virgin olive oil
    1 teaspoon shallots, minced
    freshly ground pepper, to taste
    4 cups mixed greens, torn
    2 pears, peeled, cored, sliced
    $1/4$ pound Gorgonzola cheese, cut into slices

Place walnuts in dry skillet and turn heat to medium. Toast until walnuts begin to darken, 3 to 5 minutes. Set aside to cool. Meanwhile whisk vinegar, salt and mustard together. Slowly add the oil, drop by drop while whisking until an emulsion forms. Add remaining oil, shallots and pepper. Toss greens with dressing and divide among serving plates. Decorate with pear slices and crumbled cheese. Top with toasted walnuts.

"Something about the combination of sweet pears,
salty cheese and crunchy walnuts is magical!"

Alice Avina **La Habra High School, La Habra, CA**

Snickers Salad

Serves: 6 - 8 *Salad*

    1 (small) box instant French vanilla pudding
    1 cup milk
    4 Granny Smith apples, cored, diced
    2 bananas, peeled, sliced
    2 (large) Snickers candy bars, cut into bite-sized pieces
    8 ounces Cool Whip

Mix pudding with milk. Stir in fruit and Snickers; fold in Cool Whip and serve.

"I got this recipe from my principal, Peggy Van Dyk.
Always a favorite. Never any leftovers!"

Cari Sheridan **Grace Yokley , Ontario, CA**

Easy Potato Skillet

Serves: 6 *Vegetable/Side Dish*

    $1/2$ pound cooked ham, diced
    2 tablespoons vegetable oil
    5 cups O'Brien potatoes, frozen
    8 (large) fresh eggs
    $1/4$ cup diced green chiles

In a nonstick skillet, sauté ham lightly. Add oil and potatoes and saute until lightly browned, about 15 minutes. Break eggs into small bowl; stir in chiles and mix lightly. Add to skillet and cook, stirring until eggs are in soft curds. Increase heat to high; mix eggs and potatoes together until heated through.

"From California Fresh Egg pamphlet."

Angela Cruz-Trujillo   **Valley View High School, Moreno Valley, CA**

Poppy Seed Chicken

Serves: 6   *Chicken Entreé*

    4 chicken breasts, cooked, deboned, cubed
    1 can cream of chicken soup
    1 $1/2$ cups sour cream
    1 package Ritz crackers
    2 tablespoons poppy seeds
    6 tablespoons butter or margarine
    3 cups rice, cooked

Preheat oven to 350 degrees. Layer chicken in bottom of a casserole dish. Mix soup with sour cream and pour over chicken. Crumble crackers, mix with poppy seeds and melted butter or margarine. Spoon mixture over chicken and bake until hot, 30 to 40 minutes. Serve over hot, cooked rice.

"This recipe has been a family favorite for years. It is great for any gathering because you can make it ahead of time and bake it later."

Wanda Shelton   **Newport Harbor High School, Newport Beach, CA**

Bourbon-Bacon Scallops

Serves: 4   *Seafood Entreé*

    3 tablespoons minced onion
    2 tablespoons bourbon or bourbon flavoring
        (try cooking wines of your choice)
    2 tablespoons pure maple syrup
    1 tablespoon soy sauce
    1 tablespoon Dijon mustard
    $1/4$ teaspoon pepper
    24 (large) sea scallops (about 1 $1/2$ pounds)
    12 slices bacon (about 8 ounces)
    lemon wedges, for garnish

Combine first 6 ingredients in a large bowl, stir well. Add scallops, stirring gently to coat. Cover and marinate in refrigerator 1 hour, stirring occasionally (a Ziploc bag works well). Remove scallops from marinade; reserve marinade. Cut each slice of bacon in half and wrap 1 piece around each scallop, overlapping if necessary. Thread bacon sides of scallops onto skewers, leaving some space between scallops so bacon will cook. Place skewers on a broiler rack; broil 8 minutes or until bacon is crisp and scallops are done. Baste with reserve marinade during cooking. Garnish

Easter
Easter Basket Cupcakes
Page 96

Easter
Mounds™ Coconut Easter Basket Cake
Page 98

Cinco de Mayo
Taco
Two-zies
Page 105

Cinco de Mayo
Spicy Triangle
Tostadas
Page 106

each serving with a lemon wedge. Note: Cooking time may vary according to size of scallops.

"This is a family favorite. Great placed on a bed of rice with a fresh sauteed vegetable medley of tomato wedges, yellow and green zucchini and bell pepper for a little snap. I love the scallops on the barbecue."

Barbara Allen   **Ayala High School, Chino Hills, CA**

Breakfast Strata

Serves: 6 - 8   *Pork Entreé*

1 loaf French bread, cut into $1/2$" slices
1 cup milk
$1/2$ cup mascarpone cheese
2 ripe tomatoes, sliced
6 ounces prosciutto, thinly sliced
6 ounces fontina cheese, thinly sliced
$1/4$ cup pesto
4 (large) eggs, beaten
salt and pepper, to taste
1 cup heavy cream

The day before serving, dip bread slices in milk; gently squeeze bread. Place half of the bread in a 9" x 13" baking dish and cover with mascarpone cheese, tomatoes, prosciutto and fontina. Drizzle sparingly with pesto. Overlap remaining bread slices slightly. Beat eggs with salt and pepper and pour evenly over layers in dish. Cover and refrigerate overnight. Remove dish from refrigerator and bring to room temperature. Preheat oven to 350 degrees. Drizzle casserole with cream and bake 45 minutes to 1 hour, until puffy and browned. Serve immediately.

"Great for overnight guests. No work needed in the morning."

Liz Coleman   **Oroville High School, Oroville, CA**

Coconut Sour Cream Layer Cake

Serves: 12 - 16   *Dessert*

1 box yellow cake mix
1 $1/2$ cups sugar
1 (16 ounce) container sour cream
1 (12 ounce) package coconut
1 carton Cool Whip

Bake cake according to package directions in 2 layers. Cool, split into 4 layers (or bake in 3 layer pans). Stir sugar into sour cream until mostly dissolved. Gently fold in coconut; chill. Reserve 1 cup sour cream mixture for frosting. Spread remainder between layers. Combine reserved sour cream mixture with Cool Whip, blending until smooth. Spread on top and sides of cake. Refrigerate until ready to serve.

"This is my husband's all time favorite cake!"

Kathy Sandoz   **Mesa Junior High School, Mesa, AZ**

Easy Caramel Sticky Rolls

Serves: 6   *Dessert*

    $1/2$ cup brown sugar
    $1/2$ cup heavy whipping cream
    $1/4$ cup pecans, chopped (optional)
    2 tablespoons sugar
    1 teaspoon cinnamon
    1 (11 ounce) can refrigerated soft bread sticks

Heat oven to 350 degrees. Mix brown sugar and whipping cream in
ungreased 8" round cake pan. Sprinkle with pecans. Mix sugar and
cinnamon. Unroll bread stick dough, but do not separate into bread sticks.
Sprinkle cinnamon-sugar mixture over dough. Roll up from short end;
separate at perforations. Place coiled dough in pan. Bake 20 to 25 minutes,
until golden brown. Cool 1 to 2 minutes. Turn pan upside down onto
serving plate. Let stand, upside down, 1 minute, so caramel will drizzle.
Remove pan and serve.

*"These are so easy! The kids can help make breakfast and
everyone will love the result!"*

Jill Perry   **Mojave High School, N. Las Vegas, NV**

Lemon Curd Ice Cream Cake

Serves: 12   *Dessert*

    $1/2$ cup butter, melted, divided
    $3/4$ cup walnuts or pecans, chopped
    1 cup gingersnaps, crushed
    $1/2$ teaspoon orange peel, grated
    6 egg yolks, beaten
    1 cup sugar
    2 tablespoons cornstarch
    1 tablespoon lemon peel, grated
    1 cup + 2 tablespoons lemon juice, fresh
    $1/2$ gallon vanilla ice cream

Preheat oven to 375 degrees. In bowl, mix together $1/4$ cup melted butter
with walnuts, gingersnaps and orange peel. Press into a 9" springform pan.
Bake 10 to 12 minutes; set aside. In small bowl, beat egg yolks; set aside.
Place sugar, cornstarch, lemon peel, lemon juice and remaining $1/4$ cup
butter in saucepan. Boil 2 minutes, stirring constantly, until thickened.
Pour small amount of hot sugar/butter mixture into yolks, stirring
constantly. Return to pan and cook to boiling again; set aside to cool. Place
ice cream in large bowl. Stir to soften. Add cooled lemon curd mixture and
swirl. Pour mixture into crust. Freeze at least 3 hours before serving.

Betty Wells   **Bidwell Junior High School, Chico, CA**

Strawberry Pie

Serves: 4 - 6   *Dessert*

4 cups strawberries, washed, hulled, divided
1 cup sugar
$1/4$ teaspoon salt
3 tablespoons cornstarch
1 tablespoon lemon juice
1 pastry pie crust, baked
whipped cream

Crush 2 cups strawberries in a saucepan. Mix sugar, salt and cornstarch together and add to berries. Heat, stirring constantly, until mixture thickens. Remove from heat and add lemon juice. Let sauce cool. Arrange remaining 2 cups berries in pie shell. Spread cooled sauce over berries. Chill. Top with whipped cream before serving.

Beverly Ranger   **Carpinteria High School, Carpinteria, CA**

Lemon Scones

Makes: about 20   *Dessert*

4 cups all purpose flour
2 tablespoons baking powder
$1/4$ cup sugar
dash salt
$1/4$ pound butter or margarine, cold, cut into 8 pieces
4 tablespoons lemon peel, grated
2 (large) eggs, at room temperature
$2/3$ cup lemon yogurt
$1/2$ cup currants
1 egg mixed with 1 teaspoon water, for glaze

Preheat oven to 425 degrees. Place an oven rack in the upper third of the oven. Grease a baking sheet with shortening or nonstick cooking spray. Place flour, baking powder, sugar, salt and butter in a food processor fitted with a metal blade; or in the bowl of a mixer. Process, or mix at low speed, until mixture is in coarse crumbs. Add lemon peel, eggs, yogurt and currants; mix until thoroughly combined. Remove dough to a floured surface and pat into a ball; it will be sticky. Roll it with a floured rolling pin into a 9" circle about $3/4$" thick. Cut out rounds, squares or hearts, using a 2" cookie cutter dipped in flour. On baking sheet, place the scones about 1" apart. Continue cutting and patting out dough until all scraps are used. Brush the tops lightly with the egg glaze. Bake 7 to 9 minutes or until golden.

"The scones may be covered and held at room temperature overnight, or frozen. Reheat them at 350 degrees for 5 minutes or until hot. Cut the scones in half and serve warm with lemon curd."

Betty Rabin-Fung   **Sierra Vista Junior High School, Santa Clarita, CA**

Fourth of July/Summer

Banana Punch

Serves: 30   *Appetizers & Beverages*

4 ripe bananas, peeled, mashed
juice of 4 oranges
juice of 4 lemons
1 cup sugar
6 cups water
lemon lime soda

Mix together all ingredients except lemon lime soda. Freeze in ice cube trays. Fill large glasses $1/3$ full with frozen fruit; add soda and serve.

Jill Burnham   **Bloomington High School, Bloomington, CA**

Economy Almond Punch

Serves: 32   *Appetizers & Beverages*

1 (6 ounce) can frozen lemonade
1 (6 ounce) can frozen orange juice concentrate
1 teaspoon vanilla
1 teaspoon almond extract
1 cup sugar
1 gallon water, approximate

Combine ingredients and add water to make 1 gallon. Delicious, hot or cold.

Patsy Graves   **Bingham High School, S. Jordan, UT**

Rhubarb Slush

Serves: 10   *Appetizers & Beverages*

4 cups rhubarb, fresh or frozen, diced
4 cups water
1 $1/2$ cups sugar

If rhubarb is frozen, thaw. Bring rhubarb, water and sugar to a boil. Remove from heat; strain liquid. Freeze liquid in containers 2" to 3" in height. Serve by mixing 1 part frozen mixture to 1 part Sprite or 7-Up soda.

"Tastes great during hot summer days!"

Cheryl Moyle   **Olympus High School, Salt Lake City, UT**

Salad Roll-Ups

Serves: 15 - 20   *Appetizers & Beverages*

    2 (8 ounce) packages cream cheese
    1 tablespoon mustard
    6 (extra large) flour tortillas
    8 ounces turkey, thinly sliced
    8 ounces salami, thinly sliced
    2 cloves garlic, finely chopped
    1 red onion, finely chopped
    $1/4$ cup black olives, chopped
    $1/4$ cup fresh basil leaves, finely chopped
    $1/2$ head iceberg or Romaine lettuce, shredded
    6 Roma tomatoes seeded
    1 bunch parsley, stems removed

With an electric mixer, beat cream cheese to spreadable consistency. Spread tortilla thickly with cream cheese and a layer of mustard. Cover tortilla with slices of turkey and salami. Add generous layer of mixed vegetables. Roll tortilla into a tight log, beginning from far side and being sure to retain the vegetables within the roll. Wrap roll carefully in aluminum foil and chill thoroughly. Remove foil and slice into pinwheels 1" thick. Secure each with a colored toothpick or place against each other on serving platter.

"This is a wonderful make ahead and take it dish.
Great for outdoor entertaining or potlucks. Never any leftovers!"

Pam Bonilla   **Valley View High School, Moreno Valley, CA**

Bow Tie Pasta Salad

Serves: 6 - 8   *Salad*

    1 box bow-tie pasta
    fresh basil
    2 to 3 cloves garlic, minced
    5 plum tomatoes, seeded, chopped
    2 to 4 tablespoons olive oil
    salt and pepper, to taste
    $1/4$ to $1/2$ cup Parmesan cheese, freshly grated

Cook pasta according to package directions; drain and set aside. Wash basil and dry in several layers of paper towels. Tear leaves off, discarding stems. In large bowl, combine pasta, basil and garlic and tomatoes; toss gently to combine. Add olive oil, salt and pepper to taste. Sprinkle with Parmesan cheese and toss again.

"Adjust ingredients depending on taste. A hit at potlucks!"

Irene Armijo   **Walter Johnson Junior High School, Las Vegas, NV**

Cherry Coke Salad

Serves: 10 - 12   *Salad*

2 (3 ounces) packages cherry jello
1 package gelatin
1 cup boiling water
1 (12 ounce) can cola
1 (6 ounce) can crushed pineapple
2 cups fresh bing cherries, pitted
$1/2$ cup pecans, if desired

Dissolve jello and gelatin in boiling water. Drain juice from pineapple, reserving juice. Stir cola into juice and add enough water to make 3 cups. Stir liquid into jello mixture and chill until slightly thickened. Fold in pineapple, cherries and pecans. Refrigerate until firm. Note: This can be served with or without whipped cream!

"A favorite that my mom always made with bing cherries in season. She kept out of her way by doing the most important part...pitting the cherries! Everyone loves this different, refreshing summer salad."

Karen Tilson   **Poly High School, Riverside, CA**

Jasmine Rice Salad

Serves: 6   *Salad*

3 tablespoons lemon juice
3 tablespoons olive oil
1 scant teaspoon kosher salt
2 teaspoons chili garlic sauce
2 teaspoons honey
1 teaspoon white wine vinegar
$1/4$ teaspoon garlic, crushed
$1/4$ teaspoon black pepper
2 cups jasmine rice, cooked
$3/4$ cup coconut, shredded
$1/2$ cup green onion, sliced
$1/4$ green bell pepper, roasted, diced
$1/4$ red bell pepper, roasted, diced
$1/4$ orange bell pepper, roasted, diced
$1/4$ yellow bell pepper, roasted, diced
$1/2$ cup fresh cilantro, roughly chopped
1 (small) cucumber, diced
$1/2$ cup alfalfa sprouts, roughly chopped

In a small bowl, combine lemon juice, olive oil, salt, chili garlic sauce, honey, vinegar, garlic and black pepper; whisk thoroughly and set aside to rest. Combine rice, remaining ingredients, and mix well. Pour dressing over salad to moisten ingredients and toss well. Note: If rice is prepared ahead, add a small amount of oil to help it from sticking together.

Karen Calonico   **Westmoor High School, Daly City, CA**

Pesto Couscous Salad

Serves: 4 - 6   *Salad*

1 box couscous
4 tablespoons pesto sauce, prepared
2 tablespoons water
1 teaspoon lime juice, fresh
15 cherry tomatoes
1 can garbanzo beans
2 ounces feta cheese, crumbled

Prepare couscous according to package directions; omit oil. Let chill 30 minutes. Meanwhile, mix pesto sauce with water and lime juice; let sit 10 minutes. Chop cherry tomatoes in half. Combine couscous with garbanzo beans and pesto mixture; mix well. Add tomatoes and cheese and serve.

"My family loves this salad. The pesto sauce gives it a great flavor!"
Therese Peters   **Warren High School, Downey, CA**

Wild Rice Summer Salad

Serves: 12   *Salad*

1 (6 ounce) package wild rice
3/4 cup light mayonnaise
1 teaspoon white vinegar
1 teaspoon granulated sugar
salt and pepper, to taste
2 cups cooked turkey meat, cubed
1/4 cup green onions, diced
1 cup seedless red grapes
6 ounces slivered almonds, blanched

Cook rice according to package directions; remove from heat and set aside to cool. In medium bowl, whisk together mayonnaise, vinegar, sugar, salt and pepper. Stir in rice, turkey, onion and grapes until evenly coated with dressing. Cover and refrigerate for 1 to 2 hours. Sprinkle with almonds before serving.

Linda Robinson   **Royal High School, Simi Valley, CA**

All-American Baked Beans

Serves: 16 - 18   *Vegetable/Side Dish*

6 to 8 strips bacon
3 (30 ounce) cans pork 'n beans
1 1/2 teaspoons chili powder
1 1/2 teaspoons dry mustard
1 cup brown sugar
3/4 cup molasses
3/4 teaspoon liquid smoke
1 (medium) onion, finely chopped

Fry bacon until crisp; crumble. Combine remaining ingredients with bacon in slow cooker or oven and bake at 300 degrees 5 to 6 hours.

"This recipe is a must at our family BBQ!"

Joanne Montoy   **Esperanza High School, Anaheim, CA**

Roasted Potatoes

Serves: 6 - 8   *Vegetable/Side Dish*

3 pounds (small) red potatoes
1/4 cup olive oil
2 to 3 tablespoons butter, softened
1 envelope onion soup mix

Preheat oven to 400 degrees. Cut potatoes with skins in half or quarters depending on size. In a large bowl, toss potatoes with oil, butter and soup mix until well coated. Place potatoes on a jelly roll pan and spread into one layer. Roast in oven for at least 1 hour or until browned and crisp. Flip twice during cooking to ensure browning.

"Absolutely delicious. Potatoes can also be cooked on the grill. Simply wrap in foil. The crispier they are, the better they taste. Can be tossed with minced parsley before serving."

Millie Deeton   **Ayala High School, Chino Hills, CA**

Baked Barbecue Chicken Hawaiian

Serves: 4 - 5   *Chicken Entreé*

8 - 10 pieces chicken
1/2 cup soy sauce
2 tablespoons onion, grated
2 tablespoon ginger, ground
1 cup corn starch
1/2 cup margarine
2 cups pineapple chunks, drained
1/4 cup lemon juice

Place chicken in a large bowl. Combine soy sauce, onion and ginger; pour over chicken. Let stand at least 30 minutes, turning to coat all sides. Preheat oven to 425 degrees. Drain chicken; reserve marinade. Coat chicken pieces with cornstarch. Place margarine in a shallow baking pan. Set in oven until margarine is melted. Place chicken in pan, skin side down. Bake 30 minutes or until bottom is well browned. Turn chicken over. Combine pineapple with liquid, lemon juice, and reserved marinade. Pour over chicken and bake 15 to 20 minutes longer, until tender.

Jill Burnham   Bloomington High School, Bloomington, CA

Turkey Breast Marinade

Makes: 7 - 8 cups   *Chicken Entreé*

15 ounces peanut or canola oil
15 ounces soy sauce
2 tablespoons lemon juice
2 tablespoons horseradish sauce
$1/2$ teaspoon garlic salt
32 ounces 7-Up
turkey breast or boneless chicken breasts, sliced

In a blender mix together oil, soy sauce, lemon juice, horseradish and garlic salt. Add 7-Up, a little at a time, so it doesn't foam over. Pour marinade over poultry to cover and allow to stand at least 12 hours, refrigerated. Broil or grill until lightly browned.

Jeanette Atkinson   Brinley Middle School, Las Vegas, NV

Gerry's Fabulous Marinade

Serves: 8   *Beef Entreé*

$2/3$ cup oil
$1/2$ cup lemon juice or vinegar
$1/4$ cup soy sauce
1 tablespoon Worcestershire sauce
1 to 2 cloves garlic, minced
1 teaspoon salt
$1/4$ teaspoon pepper
1 tablespoon dry mustard
$1/2$ teaspoon each: celery salt, thyme, oregano and rosemary
1 flank steak OR 8 chicken breasts OR 1 turkey breast,
    cut into 1" slices

Mix all ingredients except meat together in a large mixing bowl. Add meat; turning to coat with marinade. Cover with plastic wrap or a tight fitting lid; refrigerate 6 to 10 hours, turning meat 2 to 3 times. Cook meat on grill or under broiler until desired doneness. Serve while hot.

"Makes great sandwiches. To slice flank steak, place on clean cutting board and cut diagonally across the muscle grain in thin strips."

Anne Hawes   Cottonwood High School, Salt Lake City, UT

Julie's 4th of July BBQ Ribs

Serves: 6 - 8   *Beef Entreé*

1 rack baby back pork ribs
3 cups apple juice
$1/2$ cup apple cider vinegar
$1/2$ teaspoon garlic powder
1 (16 ounce) jar barbecue sauce
2 teaspoons garlic, minced
$1/2$ cup brown sugar

Parboil ribs in apple juice, cider vinegar and garlic powder about 45 minutes. Place ribs in a 9" x 12" baking dish and cover with barbecue sauce, minced garlic and brown sugar. Bake at 350 degrees for 30 to 40 minutes.

Bonnie Landin   **Garden Grove High School, Garden Grove, CA**

Asian Grilled Salmon

Serves: 6 - 8   *Seafood Entreé*

1 side fresh salmon, boned, skin on (about 3 pounds)
2 tablespoons Dijon mustard
3 tablespoons soy sauce
6 tablespoons olive oil
$1/2$ teaspoon garlic, minced

Light charcoal briquettes in a grill and brush grilling rack with oil to keep salmon from sticking. While grill is heating, lay salmon, skin-side down, on a cutting board and cut it crosswise into 6 equal pieces. Whisk together mustard, soy sauce, olive oil and garlic in a small bowl. Drizzle half of the marinade onto salmon and allow to sit for 10 minutes. Place salmon, skin side down on hot grill; discard marinade covering fish. Grill 4 to 5 minutes, depending on thickness of fish. Turn carefully with wide spatula and grill another 4 to 5 minutes. Salmon will be slightly raw in center, but don't worry - it will keep cooking as it sits. Transfer to a flat dish, skin side down, and spoon reserved marinade on top. Allow fish to rest 10 minutes. Remove skin and serve warm, at room temperature or chilled.

Millie Deeton   **Ayala High School, Chino Hills, CA**

Apple Fruit Cobbler

Serves: 8 - 12   *Dessert*

4 cups fresh fruit (apples or peaches), cored, peeled, sliced
2 cups sugar, divided
$1/2$ cup butter or margarine
1 cup flour
$3/4$ cup milk
2 teaspoons baking powder
dash salt

Preheat oven to 375 degrees. Combine prepared fruit with 1 cup sugar; set aside. Melt butter or margarine in a 9" x 13" pan. In mixing bowl combine flour, remaining 1 cup sugar, milk, baking powder and salt. Pour batter over melted butter in pan. Spoon fruit over top of batter. Bake 40 to 45 minutes.

"Quick and easy recipe - great when there is an abundance of fruit.
Great served warm with ice cream."

Elizabeth Thornburg   **Selma High School, Selma, CA**

Best Raspberry Ice Cream

Makes: 2 quarts   *Dessert*

3 ounces raspberry jello
$1/2$ cup boiling water
$2/3$ cup sugar
2 teaspoons vanilla
2 cups milk
2 cups cream
1 cup half & half
1 (3 ounce) package vanilla instant pudding
10 ounces frozen raspberries

Dissolve jello in boiling water. Add remaining ingredients, except raspberries and stir well. Stir in berries. Freeze in ice cream freezer. Note: This also works well with strawberry and peach flavored jello and fruit.

"This is the smoothest, creamiest ice cream ever tasted.
Always a family favorite for every summer party."

Carol Winter   **Hillcrest High School, Midvale, UT**

Caramel Crispy Ice Cream Squares

Serves: 12   *Dessert*

    1 cup butter or margarine
    $1/2$ cup brown sugar
    1 cup Rice Krispies
    1 cup coconut
    1 cup nuts, chopped
    $1/2$ gallon vanilla ice cream (in square box)
    1 jar caramel ice cream topping

Melt butter or margarine in saucepan with sugar. Cool and stir in Rice Krispies, coconut and and nuts. Press half of mixture into bottom of a 9" x 13" pan. Cut ice cream into slices and arrange over mixture in pan. Top with remaining Rice Krispies mixture and freeze until firm. Serve with caramel topping.

    "Great make-ahead dessert for a hot summer afternoon."
Ann Mohr   **Cyprus High School, Magna, UT**

Chocolate Pudding Cake

Makes: 24 bars   *Dessert*

    1 (3.5 ounce) Cook 'N Serve chocolate pudding
    2 cups milk
    1 package chocolate cake mix
    1 cup chocolate chips
    1 cup walnuts or pecans, chopped

Preheat oven to 350 degrees. Butter a 9" x 13" pan. Mix pudding with milk in medium saucepan. Bring to a boil. Turn off heat and stir in cake mix; mix well (may be a little lumpy). Spread in pan. Sprinkle with chocolate chips and nuts. Bake 25 minutes.

    "This was brought to a teacher potluck and has become the family dessert for all occasions. Super simple and quick to make."
Betty Jo Hardenbrook   **Salida Middle School, Salida, CA**

Funnel Cakes

Makes: 4 - 5   *Dessert*

    2 eggs, beaten
    1 $1/2$ cups milk
    $1/4$ cup brown sugar
    2 cups all-purpose flour
    1 $1/2$ teaspoons baking powder
    $1/4$ teaspoon salt
    2 cups cooking oil
    powdered sugar, for dusting

In a large mixing bowl, stir together eggs, milk and brown sugar, In another bowl combine flour, baking powder, and salt. Add flour mixture to egg mixture. Beat until smooth. In an 8" skillet, heat cooking oil to medium high heat (360 degrees). Fill a glass measuring cup with batter; pour batter into hot oil. Start at center of skillet and move the cup in a circular motion to form a spiral. Cook 2 1/2 minutes or until golden brown. Using 2 wide spatulas, carefully turn funnel cake. Cook about one minute more. Drain on paper towels. Dust with powdered sugar and/or fruit toppings.

"Students love making funnel cakes."

Diane Lizardi   Downey High School, Downey, CA

Great American Brownie Cherry Pie

Serves: 8 - 10   *Dessert*

1/3 cup Maraschino cherries, well drained
1/2 cup butter or margarine, softened
3/4 cup sugar

| *Photo on* |
| *back cover* |

2 eggs
2 tablespoons light corn syrup
2 teaspoons almond extract
2/3 cup all-purpose flour
1/3 cup Hershey's Cocoa or Hershey's Dutch Processed Cocoa
1/4 teaspoon baking powder
1/3 cup almonds, coarsely chopped, slivered
1 cup Hershey's Premier White Chips
non-dairy whipped topping
Maraschino cherries with stems, well drained, for garnish

Heat oven to 325 degrees. Grease and flour 9" round glass pie plate. Lightly press cherries between layers of paper towels to remove excess moisture. In large bowl, beat butter, sugar, eggs, corn syrup and almond extract until blended. Add flour, cocoa and baking powder; beat until combined. Stir in reserved chopped cherries, almonds and white chips. Pour batter into prepared pan. Bake 30 to 35 minutes or until set. Cool completely in pan or on wire rack. Cover; refrigerate until serving time. Garnish with whipped topping and cherries.

Hershey Foods   Hershey, PA

Great American Chocolate Cherry Cake

Serves: 10 - 12   *Dessert*

$2/3$ cup butter or margarine, softened
1 $3/4$ cups sugar
2 eggs
1 teaspoon each almond and vanilla extracts
1 $3/4$ cup all-purpose flour
$3/4$ cups Hershey's Dutch Processed Cocoa or Hershey's Cocoa
1 $1/2$ teaspoons baking soda
1 $1/2$ cups dairy sour cream
2 (10 ounce) jars maraschino cherries, drained, rinsed, divided
Filling:
2 cups whipping cream, cold
$1/3$ cup powdered sugar
1 teaspoon almond extract

> Photo on
> back cover

Heat oven to 350 degrees. Beat butter and sugar until creamy. Add eggs, almond and vanilla and beat until light and fluffy. Stir together flour, cocoa and baking soda; add to creamed mixture, alternately with sour cram, beating well after each addition. Pour batter into prepared pans. Bake 30 to 35 minutes or until wooden pick inserted in center comes out clean. Cool 10 minutes; remove from pans to wire racks. Cool completely. Lightly press cherries between layers of paper towels to remove excess moisture. Prepare whipped cream filling: In large bowl, beat whipping cream with powdered sugar and almond extract until stiff. Place one layer of cake, rounded side down, on serving plate; spread with $1/2$" layer of whipped cream. Reserve 12 cherries; place remaining cherries over top. Place second layer, rounded side up, on top of cherries; spread and garnish top with remaining whipped cream. Cover; refrigerate until serving time. Garnish with reserved cherries.

Hershey Foods   **Hershey, PA**

Homemade Vanilla Ice Cream

Makes: 1 gallon   *Dessert*

1 tablespoon vanilla
2 (14 ounce) cans sweetened condensed milk
4 eggs, beaten
$3/4$ cup sugar
pinch salt
$1/2$ gallon whole milk
squeeze of lemon

Blend all ingredients together in electric mixer and freeze until completely frozen through.

Deanna Lee   **Marina High School, Huntington Beach, CA**

Latin American Sugar Cookies

Makes: 3 dozen   *Dessert*

   $1/2$ cup butter or margarine
   $1/2$ cup shortening
   1 $1/4$ cups granulated sugar, divided
   1 egg yolk
   1 teaspoon vanilla
   1 teaspoon dried orange rind
   2 $1/2$ cups all-purpose flour
   $1/2$ teaspoon ground cinnamon
   dash salt
   $1/2$ cup chocolate sprinkles

Preheat oven to 275 degrees. In a large bowl, cream butter or margarine
with shortening and $3/4$ cup sugar until fluffy. Beat in egg yolk, vanilla and
orange rind. In another bowl, combine flour, cinnamon and salt. Gradually
add to creamed mixture, beating well until blended. Sprinkle remaining $1/2$
cup sugar on a piece of waxed paper. For each cookie, roll dough into a ball
the size of a small walnut. Roll in sugar until completely coated. Place balls
of cookie dough about 2" apart on greased baking sheet. grease bottom of
glass, dip in sugar and press each cookie down to about $1/2$" thickness.
Sprinkle centers with chocolate sprinkles. Bake 20 minutes, then raise
temperature of oven to 350 degrees. Bake 8 to 10 minutes more or until
lightly browned. Let cookies cool on cookie sheets for 4 minutes. Carefully
remove cookies to a plate to cool thoroughly.

Jill Marsh   **Warren High School, Downey, CA**

Red, White & Blue Cheesecake

Serves: 12   *Dessert*

   2 (8 ounce) packages cream cheese
   $2/3$ cup sugar
   2 eggs
   2 tablespoons lemon juice
   2 tablespoons vanilla
   12 vanilla wafers
   $1/2$ can each blueberry and cherry pie filling

Soften cream cheese in a 1 quart bowl in microwave for 1 $1/2$ minutes at
MEDIUM setting. Beat in sugar, eggs, lemon juice and vanilla until light and
fluffy. Line micro-muffin pan with paper liners or use custard cups with
paper lining. Place a vanilla wafer in the bottom of each liner and fill $3/4$ full
with cream cheese mixture. Cook on MEDIUM in microwave for 2 minutes,
rotating dish once. Top each with 2 tablespoons pie filling. Chill until set.

Donna Small   **Santana High School, Santee, CA**

Tin Can Ice Cream

Makes: 3 cups   *Dessert*

   1 cup milk
   1 cup whipping cream
   $1/2$ cup sugar
   $1/2$ teaspoon vanilla extract
   nuts or fruits, as desired
   You will need: (1) 1-pound coffee can with tight-fitting lid,
        (1) 3-pound coffee can with (2) tight-fitting lids
        (one for the top and one for the bottom),
        rock salt and crushed ice.

Put all ingredients in 1-pound coffee can; secure lid. Place can inside 3-pound coffee can and pack larger can with crushed ice around smaller can. Pour at least $3/4$ cup rock salt evenly over ice. Place lids on top and bottom of 3-pound can so it rolls evenly. Roll back and forth on cement slab for 10 minutes. Open 3-pound can and remove 1 pound can. Wipe off plastic lid to prevent salt water from mixing into ingredients. Open 1-pound can and stir ingredients; scraping sides of can. Replace lid. Drain salt water from larger can, add more ice and rock salt and repeat rolling for 5 minutes longer.

"Fun activity for our kids on a hot summer day!"

Pat Smith   **Kern Valley High School, Lake Isabella, CA**

Any Special Occasion

Dragon Mouth Salsa

Serves: 6 - 8 *Appetizers & Beverages*

1 (4 ounce) can black olives, chopped
1 (4 ounce) can green chiles, chopped
2 to 3 green onions, with tops, chopped
2 to 3 (large) tomatoes, seeded, chopped
1 tablespoon olive oil
2 teaspoons vinegar
2 teaspoons fresh lime juice
1 clove garlic, minced
$1/4$ cup cilantro, chopped
salt and pepper, to taste

Combine all ingredients and allow to stand about one hour to blend flavors. Adjust seasonings as needed. Serve with tortilla chips.

> *"I like to make this when my husband's home-grown tomatoes are ripe, but it's delicious with the store-bought varieties too!"*

Laura de la Motte   **Turlock High School, Turlock, CA**

Grandma Zerpoli Baked Brie

Serves: 8 *Appetizers & Beverages*

1 sheet puff pastry, thawed
1 to 2 tablespoons sweet honey mustard
$1/4$ teaspoon olive oil
$1/2$ teaspoon garlic powder
1 (8 to 10 ounce) wheel brie, chilled
2 egg whites
almonds, sliced
crackers or sliced bread, for serving

Heat oven to 375 degrees. On a floured surface, roll pastry into 12" square. Cut out two circles: one 4" to 5", one 8" to 9". Spread mustard and olive oil over each circle, leaving $1/2$" border. Sprinkle with garlic powder. Center brie on larger pastry circle. Place small pastry circle on top and brush with egg whites and olive oil. Fold bottom circle sides up and press onto top circle; sealing edges. Bake on greased cookie sheet, again brushing with egg whites. Press almonds onto sides and bake 35 minutes. Allow to stand 10 minutes before serving. Serve with crackers or bread.

> *"A very great appetizer for family get togethers or Christmas parties."*

Laura Zerpoli-Steslicki   **Monrovia High School, Monrovia, CA**

Maui Artichoke & Crab Dip

Makes: 1 quart   *Appetizers & Beverages*

2 loaves King's Hawaiian Bread
3 (8 ounce) packages cream cheese, softened
1 cup mayonnaise
$1/3$ cup Dijon mustard
$3/4$ teaspoon cayenne pepper
3 cloves garlic, minced
2 (14 ounce) cans artichoke hearts, drained, chopped
12 ounces crab meat, cooked
8 ounces cheddar cheese, shredded

Hollow one loaf of bread, leaving 1" on sides and bottom; cube removed bread and additional loaf. Mix cream cheese, mayonnaise, mustard, cayenne pepper and garlic until smooth. Fold in chopped, drained artichoke hearts and crab meat. Warm mixture in microwave. Mix half of the cheese into mixture and pour into hollowed loaf. Garnish with remaining cheese. Arrange bread cubes around loaf. Serve warm or cold.

"Never mind the calories...just enjoy!"

Myrna Swearingen   **Corona High School, Corona, CA**

Overnight Oil Buns

Makes: 5 dozen   *Breads/Baked Goods*

1 cup vegetable oil
3 eggs
4 cups warm water
1 $1/2$ cups sugar
1 tablespoon salt
3 teaspoons baking powder
1 package dry yeast
12 cups flour

In a very large bowl, whisk together all ingredients, except flour. With a wooden spoon, mix in flour 1 cup at a time until dough gets thick enough to handle. Start kneading the dough, adding the rest of the flour until dough is smooth but not sticky. Let rise about 5 hours. Shape dough into dinner rolls, using approximately 2 to 3 inches of dough. Place on greased cookie sheet. Cover rolls with a light towel and let rise several hours or overnight. Bake at 350 degrees until rolls are light golden brown, 20 to 25 minutes. Remove from oven and brush tops with butter.

"My Aunt Barb is the best baker I know. She has taught me a lot! Every holiday we look forward to these, straight from the oven!"

Sheri Crouse   **Rhodes Junior High School, Mesa, AZ**

Sugar-Free Blueberry Muffins

Makes: 10 - 12   *Breads/Baked Goods*

  $1/2$ cup corn oil
  $3/4$ cup milk
  1 egg
  1 teaspoon vanilla
  2 cups all-purpose flour
  $1/2$ cup Splenda
  1 tablespoon baking powder
  $1/2$ teaspoon salt
  1 cup fresh or frozen blueberries (do not defrost if frozen)
  1 teaspoon lemon rind, grated
  $1/2$ cup walnuts, chopped (optional)

Preheat oven to 400 degrees. Spray muffin cup with nonstick cooking spray. Combine corn oil, milk, egg and vanilla in small mixing bowl; mix until blended. Combine remaining ingredients in large mixing bowl. Make a well in center of dry ingredients and add liquid ingredients. Stir until you see just a little of the dry ingredients in the batter. Do not overmix. Fill muffin cups $2/3$ full. Bake about 20 minutes or until lightly browned and toothpick inserted in center of muffin comes out clean.

> *"This recipe is from a cookbook I wrote and dedicated to my husband, Dennis, who has Type 2 diabetes."*

Mary Lou Moore   **Mira Mesa High School, San Diego, CA**

Italian Wedding Soup

Serves: 4 - 6   *Soups*

  Meatballs:
  $1/2$ pound extra lean ground beef
  1 egg, lightly beaten
  2 tablespoons bread crumbs
  1 tablespoon Parmesan cheese, grated
  $1/2$ teaspoon fresh basil, chopped
  $1/2$ teaspoon onion powder
  $1/2$ teaspoon garlic powder
  pinch salt and pepper
  Soup:
  6 cups chicken broth
  1 tablespoon olive oil
  3 cups fresh spinach and/or escarole OR 1 cup frozen spinach
  1 teaspoon fresh basil, chopped
  $3/4$ cup Orzo, uncooked
  1 teaspoon garlic, finely chopped
  $1/2$ cup carrot, finely chopped
  $1/2$ cup celery, finely chopped

Mix meatball ingredients together by hand. Shape into tiny meatballs. Bake at 250 degrees for 45 minutes (or pan fry in olive oil for crispier exterior). In saucepan, heat broth to a boil. Stir in cooked meatballs and remaining ingredients. Return to boil. Reduce heat to medium. Cook at a slow boil 10 minutes or until Orzo is tender, stirring frequently. Serve sprinkled with cheese. Note: To make this a quick recipe, you can use frozen meatballs from the market. If they are large, follow cooking directions and cut in half before adding to soup.

"I got this recipe from our close friends, Vic and Sandy Puglisi. It's one you want to try. It's excellent and very filling."

Connie Sweet   **Rim of the World High School, Lake Arrowhead, CA**

"Tony Roma's" Baked Potato Soup

Serves: 6 - 8   *Soups*

  2 (medium) potatoes, (about 2 cups) chopped
  3 tablespoons butter
  1 cup white onion, diced
  2 tablespoons flour
  4 cups chicken stock
  2 cups water
  $1/4$ cup cornstarch
  1 $1/2$ cups instant mashed potatoes
  1 teaspoon salt
  $3/4$ teaspoon pepper
  $1/2$ teaspoon basil
  $1/8$ teaspoon thyme
  1 cup half & half
  Garnishes:
  $1/2$ cup cheddar cheese, shredded
  $1/4$ cup cooked bacon, crumbled
  2 green onions, chopped (green part only)

Preheat oven to 400 degrees and bake potatoes for 1 hour or until done; remove and cool. As potatoes cool, prepare soup by melting butter in large saucepan. Saute onion until light brown. Add flour to onions and stir, making a roux. Add chicken stock, water, cornstarch, instant mashed potatoes, and spices to saucepan and bring to a boil. Reduce heat and simmer 5 minutes. Cut baked potatoes in half lengthwise and scoop out contents with a large spoon; discard skins. Chop potatoes into $1/2$" chunks. Carefully add potato chunks along with half & half to saucepan; bring soup back to a boil, then reduce heat and simmer 15 minutes, or until thick. To serve, spoon into soup bowls and top each serving with 1 tablespoon shredded cheese, $1/2$ tablespoon bacon and a teaspoon of green onion.

Mary Tatro-Davis   **Lakeview Junior High School, Orcutt, CA**

Meg's Artichoke Heart & Rice Salad

Serves: 4 - 6   *Salad*

1 package chicken Rice-A-Roni
2 jars marinated artichoke hearts, with liquid, chopped
1 cup mayonnaise
1 cup water chestnuts, diced
dash curry, to taste
salt and pepper, to taste
1 pound (medium) shrimp, cooked (or chicken), cooked, diced

Prepare Rice-A-Roni according to package directions. Add artichoke hearts, including liquid, mayonnaise, water chestnuts, curry, salt and pepper, and shrimp or chicken. Serve chilled. Note: For variety, you can add chopped celery, cucumbers or onion as extra ingredients.

"Our daughter, Katie's, sorority sisters from Berkeley join us every Memorial Day for river rafting. One of them, Meg, wouldn't share this salad with the rest of us. Now I make one salad for Meg and one salad for the rest of us! You'll love it too!"

Brenda Burke   **Mt. Whitney High School, Visalia, CA**

Peg's Salad

Serves: 8   *Salad*

1 (15 ounce) can crushed pineapple
1 (large) package lemon jello
8 ounces cream cheese, cut into cubes
1 (12 ounce) can evaporated milk, well chilled
2/3 cup celery, finely chopped
2/3 cup nuts, finely chopped

Drain crushed pineapple, reserving juice. Heat drained juice and dissolve the jello. Stir in cream cheese and mix until smooth. Place in refrigerator until chilled and thick. Place mixer bowl, beaters and evaporated milk in refrigerator until well chilled. Whip evaporated milk until thick. Spoon jello mixture in small amounts into whipped milk. Fold in pineapple, celery and nuts. Pour into serving dish.

"My 6th grade teacher, Mrs. Murphy, shared her daughter's favorite salad recipe...her name was Peggy...thus the name...a family favorite."

Joyce Doig   **Ranchero Middle School, Hesperia, CA**

Spicy Asian Slaw

Serves: 4   *Salad*

3 tablespoons rice vinegar
2 tablespoons soy sauce
1 tablespoon Asian sesame oil
$1/4$ teaspoon hot pepper flakes
4 cups OR 1 (8 ounce) package coleslaw mix
    (shredded fresh cabbage mix and carrots)
$1/3$ cup scallions, thinly sliced
$1/4$ to $1/2$ cup raisins
$1/4$ cup peanuts or cashews, chopped

Whisk together vinegar, soy sauce, sesame oil and red pepper flakes in a
large bowl. Add coleslaw mix, scallions and raisins; toss well. Chill at least
1 hour or up to 24 hours before serving. Sprinkle with nuts before serving.

"A great, low-calorie salad. Quick and easy to prepare!"

Diane Wolak   **Martin Luther King High School, Riverside, CA**

Strawberry Romaine Salad with Raspberry Poppy Seed Dressing

Serves: 8 - 10   *Salad*

2 heads romaine lettuce, washed, dried, torn into bite-sized pieces
1 pint fresh strawberries, sliced
2 cups mayonnaise
$1/3$ cup half & half or milk
2 tablespoons poppy seeds
$2/3$ cup sugar
$1/2$ cup raspberry vinegar
3 tablespoons raspberry jam
$1/2$ cup almonds, toasted, slivered

Toss romaine and strawberries together; set aside. In blender, mix together
mayonnaise, half & half or milk, poppy seeds, sugar, vinegar and jam; mix
well. Pour over lettuce and toss well. Top with almonds and serve.

"This dressing will keep in the refrigerator for one week."

Vicki Pearl   **Townsend Junior High School, Chino Hills, CA**

Brown & White Rice Casserole

Serves: 6   *Vegetable/Side Dish*

6 slices bacon, chopped
$1/2$ pound mushrooms, sliced
4 green onions, sliced
6 tablespoons butter, divided
$1/4$ cup slivered almonds
$3/4$ cup quick cooking brown rice
$3/4$ cup quick cooking white rice
$1/4$ teaspoon salt
$1/4$ teaspoon pepper
$1/4$ teaspoon thyme
$1/4$ teaspoon marjoram
3 $1/4$ cups beef broth
2 tablespoons Parmesan cheese, shredded

Saute bacon until crisp; drain and place in 2 $1/2$ quart casserole. Saute mushrooms and onions in 2 tablespoons butter; add to bacon in dish. Saute and toast almonds with brown and white rice in 3 tablespoons butter; add to dish. Toss in seasonings. Bring beef broth to a boil and pour over rice mixture, stirring well. Cover and bake 40 minutes. Uncover, stir and dot with 1 tablespoon butter. Sprinkle with cheese. Cover and bake 10 minutes more.

"From a friend and great cook, Myrna Patane.
Excellent for company! This dish cooks while you entertain!"

Liz Coleman   **Oroville High School, Oroville, CA**

Gulliver's Corn

Serves: 8 - 10   *Vegetable/Side Dish*

1 (20 ounce) bag frozen corn
$1/2$ pint whipping cream
8 ounces milk
1 teaspoon salt
2 tablespoons sugar
pinch pepper
2 tablespoons butter, melted
2 tablespoons flour

In medium saucepan, place corn, whipping cream, milk, salt, sugar and pepper; bring to a boil. Boil 5 minutes, stirring occasionally. Melt butter and gradually stir in flour. Stir into corn mixture until thickened. Serve.

Pamela Campion   **Dublin High School, Dublin, CA**

Chicken 'n Dumplings

Serves: 6 - 8   *Chicken Entreé*

1 whole chicken
4 cups water
1 rib celery
1 onion
2 teaspoons salt, divided
pinch pepper
1 cup flour
3/4 teaspoon celery salt
1/8 teaspoon baking powder
2 tablespoons margarine, melted
1 egg, beaten
3 tablespoons milk

In a large pot, place chicken, water, celery, onion, 1 teaspoon salt and pepper. Heat to boiling and simmer 45 minutes; cool. Debone and cut chicken into bite-sized pieces. Strain the broth. Make dumplings by combining flour, remaining 1 teaspoon salt, celery salt, baking powder, melted margarine, egg and milk; roll out and cut into strips. Bring broth to a boil and drop in dumplings. Simmer 20 minutes. Add chicken and heat through. Serve at once.

"Serve this homemade hot soup with hot rolls or bread sticks."

Laurie deJong   **Bingham High School, So. Jordan, UT**

Jerk Chicken with Mango Salsa

Serves: 6 - 12   *Chicken Entreé*

Chicken Rub: (begin 12 to 48 hours ahead of grilling time)
2 chiles (habañero, scotch bonnets, or jalapeños)
2 scallions, chopped
2 tablespoons soy sauce
2 tablespoons fresh lime juice
5 teaspoons allspice
3 teaspoons dry mustard
2 cloves garlic
1 tablespoon salt
2 teaspoons sugar
1 $1/2$ teaspoons dried thyme
1 teaspoon cinnamon
1 package chicken breasts, boneless, skinless
2 packages chicken thighs
Mango Salsa:
1 sweet onion (Walla Walla, Texas 100, Maui or large white)
2 mangoes
$1/4$ cup fresh lime juice
pinch salt
1 tablespoon honey
fresh basil, mint or cilantro

Prepare chicken rub: Using rubber gloves, remove seeds from chiles. Chop and place in food processor. Add remaining "rub" ingredients and blend until fine. Rub paste over chicken pieces (don't forget those gloves). Place in Ziploc bags and marinate up to 48 hours, turning bags occasionally. Prepare salsa in morning or one day ahead: Slice onions into thick slices. Brush with olive oil, sprinkle with salt and pepper. Grill 10 to 15 minutes per side. (Place onions on a piece of heavy duty aluminum foil with holes poked in it...that way they don't fall through the grill.) Chop cooked onions. Peel and chop mangoes and add to onion. Add remaining ingredients,

"This recipe is great for a spring or summer barbecue. It always gets rave reviews! Being able to start the chicken 1 to 2 days before gives you a head start and makes things easier on the special day you serve it!"

Debbie Powers   **Griffiths Middle School, Downey, CA**

Chile Con Carne

Serves: 4   *Beef Entreé*

1 $1/2$ pounds ground beef
$1/4$ cup onion, chopped
$1/2$ cup green pepper, chopped
1 $1/2$ cups water
1 (28 ounce) can whole tomatoes
1 teaspoon salt
$1/2$ teaspoon paprika
1 teaspoon chili powder
1 (16 ounce) can kidney beans, well drained

Brown meat and onions in a pressure cooker. Add remaining ingredients, except beans. Cover, set control and cook 10 minutes after control jiggles. Reduce pressure normally for 5 minutes, then place under faucet. Add kidney beans and simmer a few minutes. Note: This can also be made in a crockpot. Brown the meat with onions in a skillet, then add to crockpot, along with remaining ingredients, except beans. Cook 7 to 10 hours. Stir beans in the last 30 minutes of cooking to heat through.

"Double, triple or quadruple to accommodate the number of guests."
Rita Urquidi   **Nogales High School, La Puente, CA**

Pork Tenderloin with Port-Cherry Sauce

Serves: 6   *Pork Entreé*

$2/3$ cup port or sweet red wine
$3/4$ cup dried tart cherries
3 tablespoons flour
$1/4$ teaspoon pepper
$1/2$ teaspoon ground coriander
$1/4$ teaspoon salt
1 $1/2$ pounds pork tenderloin
1 tablespoon butter
2 tablespoons shallots, finely chopped
1 cup chicken broth

Microwave port or sweet red wine 20 seconds on HIGH to get it very warm. Pour over cherries; cover and let stand 10 minutes to soften. Drain, reserving wine. In a shallow dish, combine flour, pepper, coriander and salt. Dredge pork in this mixture. Melt butter in a large heavy skillet over medium heat. Add pork, cooking 3 minutes on each side or until browned. Remove pork, stir in reserved wine, scraping pan to loosen any browned bits. Add softened cherries and shallots. Reduce heat and cook 3 minutes, stirring frequently. Add broth and bring to a simmer. Return pork to pan.

Partially cover and cook 10 minutes. Uncover and cook 12 minutes more, or until a meat thermometer registers 155 degrees, turning pork occasionally. Cut into slices and serve with sauce.

"This is deceivingly simple but very elegant. To round out the menu, I saute fresh spinach with garlic, bake some sweet potatoes and serve hot crusty rolls, along with a nice bottle of Gewurztraminer."

Margo Olsen   **Amador Valley High School, Pleasanton, CA**

Quiche Cancun

Serves: 6   ***Meatless Entreé***

1 cup evaporated milk (or $^1/_2$ cup evaporated milk
    and $^1/_2$ cup whole milk)
3 eggs
2 (large) flour tortillas
$^1/_2$ cup Monterey jack cheese, grated
$^1/_2$ cup cheddar cheese, grated
1 (small) can diced green chiles
1 (small) can olives, sliced
$^1/_2$ cup fresh salsa
Garnishes: salsa, sour cream and guacamole

Preheat oven to 400 degrees. Place milk in microwave safe dish and heat in microwave 90 seconds at MEDIUM power. Place eggs in blender and blend. Slowly add milk to blender; set aside. Place tortillas in glass pie plate (edges should extend quite a bit over the top). Sprinkle half of the cheese; half of the chiles, half of the olives and $^1/_2$ cup salsa over bottom of tortillas. Pour egg mixture over top. Sprinkle remaining ingredients over top and bake in microwave on MEDIUM 7 minutes. Remove and place in oven for 10 minutes. Cut into pie shape wedges and serve with salsa, sour cream and guacamole.

"This very attractive, colorful quiche is great for holidays. I make this for breakfast Christmas and New Year's morning or anytime that I have guests for breakfast. Also great for brunch. Everyone wants 'seconds'. No matter how much I make, it's never enough!"

Earline Paulson   **Upland High School, Upland, CA**

Carrot Cake

Serves: 8 - 10   *Dessert*

4 eggs, beaten
1 $1/4$ cup vegetable oil or butter
2 cups carrot, grated
1 (8 ounce) can crushed pineapple, drained
2 cups flour
2 teaspoons baking powder
1 $1/2$ teaspoons baking soda
1 teaspoon salt
2 teaspoons cinnamon
2 cups sugar
1 cup walnuts, chopped
Frosting:
$1/2$ cup butter
8 ounces cream cheese, softened
1 teaspoon vanilla
1 $1/2$ cups powdered sugar

Generously grease a round bundt pan with butter. Sprinkle with flour to coat butter. Heat oven to 350 degrees. Beat together eggs, oil; stir in carrot and pineapple. In another large bowl, combine flour, baking powder and soda, salt, cinnamon, sugar and walnuts. Slowly beat dry ingredients into creamed mixture, scraping the sides of the bowl; beat again. Pour into prepared pan and bake 20 minutes. Lower temperature to 325 degrees and bake another 30 minutes. Test doneness by inserting toothpick in center; it should come out clean. Remove from oven and cool. Meanwhile, beat together butter, cream cheese, vanilla and powdered sugar. Frost cooled cake.

"Alison Taylor, a very dear friend says 'This cake has made me famous! I call it the Cake of Fame.' I have had people who do not like carrot cake love this! I will honor my friend, Naoko Rickman, who gave me this recipe. Naoko has gone to be with our Lord Jesus. She worked, in her younger years, as a governess for the daughters of actors Robert Wagner and Natalie Wood."

Darlene V. Sears Brown   **Golden Valley Middle School, San Bernardino, CA**

Cherries Jubilee

Serves: 4 - 6   *Dessert*

1 orange
1 can bing cherries
2 tablespoons sugar
2 tablespoons cornstarch (optional)
$1/4$ cup cold water (optional)
$1/2$ to 1 teaspoon cherry flavoring
frozen vanilla yogurt

Remove zest from orange and place in saucepan. Cut orange in half and squeeze juice into saucepan. Stir in can of cherries, along with their juice, add sugar and heat until reduced and thickened. (If juice does not thicken enough, mix cornstarch with cold water and stir into cherry mixture, stirring rapidly and constantly; then reheat mixture until thickened and glossy.) Pour hot mixture over individual servings of frozen vanilla yogurt and sprinkle with a little sugar and few drops of cherry flavoring. Using a match, light cherry flavoring on fire and serve dessert flambe!

Nancy Eckhout   **Brighton High School, Salt Lake City, UT**

Cheese Cake with Frosting

Serves: 9 - 12   ***Dessert***

    1 box yellow cake mix
    4 eggs, divided
    1 (8 ounce) package cream cheese
    1 stick butter or margarine
    2 teaspoons vanilla
    1 pound powdered sugar
    1 cup pecans

Preheat oven to 350 degrees. Combine cake mix and 2 eggs; pat in bottom of a 9" x 13" greased pan. Beat cream cheese with butter or margarine, remaining 2 eggs, vanilla, powdered sugar and pecans. Pour over cake. Bake 35 to 40 minutes. Note: If cooking too fast, reduce heat to 325 degrees.

"Helen Ridley, a very special friend, gave this delicious
old southern recipe to me. "

Darlene V. Sears Brown   **Golden Valley Middle School, San Bernardino, CA**

Chocolate Butterscotch Squares

Makes: 24   ***Dessert***

    1 cup sugar
    1 cup Karo syrup
    1 $1/2$ cups peanut butter
    2 teaspoons vanilla
    9 cups corn flakes
    2 cups chocolate chips
    1 cup butterscotch chips

In saucepan, heat sugar and Karo syrup until dissolved. Stir in peanut butter and vanilla until melted. Measure corn flakes into large bowl. Pour warm mixture over corn flakes and stir. Spread flakes onto a buttered 9" x 13" cake pan. Over double-boiler, or in microwave, melt chocolate and butterscotch chips. Evenly pour/spread melted chips over flakes. Cool and cut into squares.

"A favorite with everyone - especially the cook - no baking needed!"

Christine Becker   **Paradise Intermediate School, Paradise, CA**

Chocolate Crinkles

Makes: 5 - 6 dozen   *Dessert*

4 (1 ounce) squares unsweetened chocolate
$^1/_2$ cup vegetable oil
2 cups sugar
4 eggs
1 teaspoon vanilla
2 cups all-purpose flour
2 teaspoons baking powder
$^1/_2$ teaspoon salt
1 cup powdered sugar

In a large bowl, melt chocolate at 1 minute intervals. Add oil and sugar; mix well. Blend in eggs, one at a time, beating well after each addition. Add vanilla. Sift in flour, baking powder and salt into chocolate mixture. Chill several hours or overnight. Preheat oven to 350 degrees. Drop teaspoonful of dough into powdered sugar. Roll around and shape into ball. Place balls 2" apart onto greased baking sheet. Bake 8 to 10 minutes. **Do not overbake.** Remove from cookie sheet immediately.

Elsie Polston   **Pioneer Middle School, Tustin, CA**

Coffee Bars

Makes: 15 - 19 bars   *Dessert*

$^1/_4$ cup shortening
1 cup brown sugar
1 egg
$^1/_2$ cup hot coffee
1 $^1/_2$ cups flour
1 teaspoon baking powder
$^1/_4$ teaspoon baking soda
$^1/_4$ teaspoon salt
$^1/_2$ teaspoon cinnamon
$^1/_2$ cup raisins (optional)
$^1/_4$ cup nuts, chopped (optional)
2 cups powdered sugar
$^1/_8$ to $^1/_4$ cup milk

Preheat oven to 350 degrees. Grease and flour a 9" x 13" pan. Mix together shortening, brown sugar, egg, coffee, flour, baking powder and soda, salt, cinnamon, raisins and nuts; spread into pan. Bake 15 to 20 minutes. Make icing by combining powdered sugar and enough milk to make a thin icing. Drizzle over coffee bars while still warm. Serve.

"Unexpected company? A batch of coffee bars for a homemade treat!"
Jackie Welch-Doubeck   **Burkholder Junior High School, Henderson, NV**

Easy Breezy Cheesecake

Serves: 8   *Dessert*

1 ¹/2 cups graham crackers, crushed

$^1/_3$ cup butter, melted

$^3/_4$ cup +6 tablespoons sugar, divided

8 ounces + 3 ounces cream cheese

2 eggs

$^1/_2$ teaspoon lemon juice

1 $^1/_2$ cups sour cream

1 teaspoon vanilla

Preheat oven to 350 degrees. Mix graham cracker crumbs with melted butter and 3 tablespoons sugar. Press firmly against bottom and sides of a 9" pie plate and bake 10 minutes or until lightly browned. Mix cream cheese, eggs, $^3/_4$ cup sugar and lemon juice on medium speed for 10 minutes. Pour filling into crust and return to oven for 20 to 25 minutes. Remove from oven and let set 10 minutes before adding topping. Mix sour cream, remaining 3 tablespoons sugar and vanilla on low speed until blended. Pour over pie and return to oven for 10 minutes more. Chill in refrigerator at least 2 hours before serving.

"Easy and less expensive than most cheesecakes.My students loved it! One of the few recipes they actually re-made at home!"

Beckie Bloemker   **Foothill High School, Sacramento, CA**

M&M Oatmeal Brownies

Makes: 5 dozen   *Dessert*

1 $^1/_2$ cups quick cooking oats

1 cup M&M miniature candies

$^1/_2$ cup flour

$^1/_2$ cup brown sugar

$^1/_2$ teaspoon baking soda

$^1/_2$ cup butter or margarine, melted

1 package fudge brownie mix

Preheat oven to 350 degrees. Combine the first 6 ingredients; mix well. Set aside a cup of mixture for topping. Pat remaining mixture into greased baking pan. Prepare brownie mix according to package directions. Spread over M&M mixture. Sprinkle with reserved M&M mixture. Bake 25 to 30 minutes. Cool and cut into squares.

"This is fun for any holiday or celebration. Everyone loves M&M's!"

Robin Ali   **Nevada Union High School, Grass Valley, CA**

Mountain High No Bake Cheesecake

Serves: 6 - 8   *Dessert*

1 envelope unflavored gelatin
$1/4$ cup boiling water
2 (8 ounce) packages cream cheese, room temperature
$1/2$ cup sugar
1 cup Mountain High vanilla yogurt
1 prepared graham cracker crust

Dissolve gelatin in boiling water. In a separate bowl, use hand mixer to blend cream cheese and sugar until smooth. Fold in yogurt and gelatin. Spoon into prepared pie crust and refrigerate 2 to 3 hours. Serve plain or topped with fruit.

"I received this recipe at a Foods show. A nice light nutritious cheesecake that requires no cooking. Cheesecake is a favorite with my students!"

Jean Adams   **Sonora High School, Sonora, CA**

New York Cheesecake

Serves: 10 - 12   *Dessert*

10 graham crackers, ($3/4$ cup) crushed
1 $1/4$ cups + 2 tablespoons sugar, divided
1 tablespoon butter, melted
4 (8 ounce) packages cream cheese, at room temperature
5 eggs
1 $1/2$ teaspoons lemon peel, grated
⁻2 teaspoons vanilla, divided
2 cups sour cream

Preheat oven to 375 degrees. Crush graham crackers; mix with 1 tablespoon sugar and melted butter. Press lightly into bottom of 9" springform pan. Refrigerate while filling is being prepared. In large bowl with electric mixer at medium speed, beat cream cheese until light. Add eggs, 1 teaspoon vanilla, lemon rind and 1 $1/4$ cups sugar. Continue beating until creamy and light. Pour into prepared crust. Bake 45 to 60 minutes. In medium bowl with wooden spoon, beat together sour cream, remaining 1 tablespoon sugar and remaining 1 teaspoon vanilla. Remove cheesecake from oven. Spread topping evenly over surface and return to oven to bake 5 minutes more. Cool in pan on wire rack. Refrigerate 5 hours or overnight. To serve, remove sides of springform pan. Cut into 10 to 12 slices.

"Great for any holiday or special occasions! Add sliced strawberries or peaches when served for special, special events!"

Nancy Phillips   **Ridgeview High School, Bakersfield, CA**

144

No-Fail Sugar Cookies

Makes: 8 dozen   *Dessert*

2 cups butter, softened
2 cups granulated sugar
2 eggs
2 teaspoons vanilla
6 cups flour
3 teaspoons baking powder
1 teaspoon salt
Royal Icing:
1 pound powdered sugar
3 tablespoons meringue powder
1 teaspoon vanilla
5 to 6 tablespoons lukewarm water
gel food colorings

In a large bowl, cream butter and sugar until well blended. Add eggs and vanilla and beat well. Mix dry ingredients together; beat thoroughly into butter mixture. Place dough in a large Ziploc bag and chill 1 to 2 hours. (Dough may be frozen at this stage for later use.) Remove a portion of dough at a time and roll to desired thickness on a floured board. Cut into desired shapes. Bake on ungreased cookie sheet at 350 degrees for 8 to 10 minutes or until just beginning to turn brown around the edges. Cool. Prepare icing by mixing together powdered sugar, meringue powder, and vanilla. Slowly add water, a tablespoon at a time, until a base consistency is reached. To make a flow consistency, add warm water, a teaspoon at a time, until icing is the consistency of heavy cream. Divide icing and add drops of desired gel coloring. (Be sure to cover icing when not using or it will harden.) Pipe on the base consistency and spread on the flow consistency icing.

"These cookies are a hit at all our festive family functions.
The fun is in collecting copper cookie cutters to fit the occasion."

Gerry Henderson   **Temple City High School, Temple City, CA**

Un-Birthday Blackberry Crisp

Serves: 9   *Dessert*

    5 to 6 cups fresh blackberries
    3/4 cup sugar
    1/2 box granola cereal, without raisins
    1 cup butter or margarine

Preheat oven to 350 degrees. Wash blackberries; stir in sugar. Pour into 9" x
9" square pan and cover with a 1" layer of granola. Cut butter or margarine
into thin slices and lay on top of granola. Bake 30 to 45 minutes, until berry
juice bubbles up through edges of granola. Serve warm with ice cream or
cold with cottage cheese or whipped cream.

"This is great for people with winter birthdays who need a
Very Merry Un-Birthday or when blackberry picking season is here."

Cyndi Matthews   **Etiwanda High School, Etiwanda, CA**

To Beg For Doggie Treats

Makes: 2 dozen   *Doggie Dessert*

3 tablespoons peanut butter
$1/2$ cup canola oil
2 (medium) eggs
$3/4$ cup water or broth
2 teaspoons vanilla
$1/2$ cup cornmeal
1 $1/2$ cups unbleached flour
1 $1/2$ cups whole wheat flour
$1/2$ cup rolled oats

Preheat oven to 400 degrees. Combine peanut butter, oil, eggs, broth, and vanilla in a bowl and whisk whisk whisk. Set aside. Combine remaining ingredients in a second bowl and stir to mix. Pour wet ingredients into dry ingredients and beat by hand or use a mixer, until dough forms a ball. Roll dough to $1/4$" thickness on a lightly floured board. Cut out using your favorite cookie cutter (mine is a dog bone). Place biscuits on baking sheets and bake 20 minutes. Turn off oven and leave biscuits in oven until cool.

"My dogs, Tucker and Dudley, beg for more!!!"

Jill Lyman   Monte Vista High School, Spring Valley, CA

Index of Contributors

CONTRIBUTORS

HOLIDAYS & PARTIES

Index by Type of Recipe

RECIPE TYPE

Miscellaneous

HOLIDAYS&PARTIES

CALIFORNIA
Cookbook
1907 Skycrest Drive
Fullerton, CA 92831

Please send me _____ copy(s) of **Holidays & Parties** at **$10.95**ea.

(includes tax and postage). Make checks payable to California Cookbook Co.

Enclosed is my check for _____ book(s) at $10.95 ea $_____.

Name _____

Address _____

City _____ State _____ Zip _____

HOLIDAYS&PARTIES

CALIFORNIA
Cookbook
1907 Skycrest Drive
Fullerton, CA 92831

Please send me _____ copy(s) of **Holidays & Parties** at **$10.95**ea.

(includes tax and postage). Make checks payable to California Cookbook Co.

Enclosed is my check for _____ book(s) at $10.95 ea $_____.

Name _____

Address _____

City _____ State _____ Zip _____

HOLIDAYS&PARTIES

CALIFORNIA
Cookbook
1907 Skycrest Drive
Fullerton, CA 92831

Please send me _____ copy(s) of **Holidays & Parties** at **$10.95**ea.

(includes tax and postage). Make checks payable to California Cookbook Co.

Enclosed is my check for _____ book(s) at $10.95 ea $_____.

Name _____

Address _____

City _____ State _____ Zip _____